May All
Who Come Behind
Us
FIND US
FAITHFUL

BOB RUSSELL

STANDARD
PUBLISHING
Cincinnati, Ohio

Library of Congress Cataloging-in-Publication Data

Russell, Bob, 1943—
    May all who come behind us find us faithful / Bob Russell.
        p.   cm.
    ISBN 0-7847-0307-8
    1. Family—Religious life. 2. Parenting—Religious aspects—
Christianity. 3. Bible—Biography. I. Title.
BV4526.2.R87   1995
248.4—dc20   94-39423
                                                              CIP

Cover design by Listenberger Design Associates.

02 01 00 99 98 97 96 95   5 4 3 2 1

Contents

Introduction 5
    Passing the Baton Is No Easy Task

Chapter 1: Demonstrate Priorities 11
    Abraham and Isaac

Chapter 2: Communicate Love 23
    Jacob and His Sons

Chapter 3: Teach Responsibility 37
    Jochebed and Miriam

Chapter 4: Cultivate Respect 49
    Eli and Hophni & Phinehas

Chapter 5: Commit to God..61
    Hannah and Samuel

Chapter 6: Develop Courage......................................71
    David

Chapter 7: Build a Friendship...................................87
    David and Jonathan

Chapter 8: Encourage Evangelism...........................99
    Naaman's Servant

Chapter 9: Foster Faithfulness 111
    Joash

Chapter 10: Nurture Giftedness 121
    Jesus

Chapter 11: Saturate With Scripture......................................135
    Timothy

Chapter 12: Instill Distinctiveness...147
    Paul's Nephew

Passing the Baton Is No Easy Task

Good relay teams spend hours practicing the passing of the baton. The runners know that dropping the baton almost always means losing the race.

It has been said that the church is always just one generation away from extinction. Adult Christians must take seriously the biblical command to pass on the baton of faith to the next generation. Like a good relay team, we must develop effective strategies for passing our faith to those who come behind us. To drop the baton is to lose the race.

Taking care to pass the baton of faith is especially important in this era because there are so many forces working against us, and more importantly, against our children. Satan is saturating our young people with concepts that are diametrically opposed to our standards. The peer pressure that teenagers face today is largely anti-Christian. They are often ridiculed by their friends if they have not had a sexual experience. They are ostracized if they don't drink, use drugs, or use vulgar language.

Too often the adults around them are doing little to alleviate that pressure.

School Systems Are Working Against Our Children

In many of our schools, our children are taught values that are contrary to the Word of God. In too many public schools, they are indoctrinated into a philosophy of moral relativism: there are no absolutes and everyone should be free to do his own thing. Tolerance is extolled as the highest virtue. You have no right, they say, to criticize someone else's culture or values.

Students are told that premarital sex is a personal choice; "Just use protection."

They are taught that the world occurred accidentally, and that life itself developed by chance through evolution.

If they graduate from high school with their values still intact, young people face even greater pressure on the university campuses. There they are often taught that homosexuality is an acceptable alternate life-style, that the Bible is a book of mythical stories, that Christianity has been harmful to the world, and that Christians are unloving and intolerant because they believe that everyone should abide by the same set of values. Facts about America's Christian heritage, Western civilization's moral roots, the historical reliability of the Bible, and scientific evidence for creation are suppressed or ignored in most schools and colleges.

The Government Is Working Against Our Children

Abraham Lincoln said, "The philosophy of the school in one generation will become the philosophy of the government in the next" It is no surprise, then, that the government is also communicating values that are anti-Christian.

Former AIDS czar Kristine Gebbie, speaking at a conference on teenage pregnancy, said, "As long as the prudish are allowed to define premarital sex in terms of don'ts and diseases, . . . we will continue to be a repressed, Victorian society that misrepresents information, denies sexuality early, denies homosexual sexuality, particularly in teens, and leave people abandoned, with no place to go" (*World Magazine*, October 30, 1993). The one whom the government had named as the top official in charge of deterring AIDS in our society pointed the finger of blame at those who believe in family values. Rather than encourage monogamy and abstinence—the surest ways to prevent AIDS—she chose to advance an immoral and deadly agenda.

William Bennett, former Secretary of Education, said, "We see the last respectable form of bigotry in America: People who urge bringing time-honored religious beliefs into public policy are now the object of scorn" (*World Magazine*, October 30, 1993).

6

The Media Is Working Against Our Children

The message our children are receiving from the media is also counter-Christian. In its first release, the movie *The Program* contained a scene in which football players lay down on the white line of a busy highway while cars screamed by them at sixty miles per hour. This daring deed was supposed to be proof of their manhood. To prove his own manhood, teenager Michael Shingledecker emulated the act. He was hit and killed. Several others have been seriously injured while trying the same thing. After being pressured by parents and concerned citizens, the producers reluctantly removed the scene from the movie.

For years, Hollywood has insisted that they don't shape values; they just reflect community standards. At the same time, thirty-second segments of television are sold to advertisers for thousands of dollars with the promise that they can change the buying habits of the American people. If behavior can be changed with thirty-second commercials, what immense power is present in two-hour feature films!

It is obvious that young people attempt to reproduce in their own lives what is glamorized on the screen. A five-year-old boy in Dayton, Ohio, set fire to his home after watching a *Beavis and Butthead* cartoon on MTV. (Those mindless cartoon characters refer to starting fires as "cool.") The fire took the life of the boy's baby sister. The parents have complained against the cable channel for encouraging playing with fire, and MTV has agreed to change that particular aspect of their cartoon. But what in the world were those parents doing, allowing their five-year-old to watch MTV? We must wake up and recognize that our adversary stalks about like a roaring lion, seeking whom he may devour! (1 Peter 5:8). Satan is effectively using the media to steal, kill, and destroy moral values in this country.

Attorney General Janet Reno has warned television producers that they must reduce the violence or the government will take censorship action. When even a liberal government begins to show concern for what is happening to our society, it is time for Christians to be alert!

We Must Develop a Strategy

We as Christians must develop an effective, proactive strategy for transferring our faith and God's ideas to those who come behind us. In this book, we will study how several biblical characters responded to their assignment to pass the faith along. Some of them were successful in transferring their faith, and some were not successful. But we can learn from both the positive and negative examples in Scripture how we can pass the baton, and how we can avoid common mistakes that could cause us to lose the race.

In Deuteronomy 11:18-21, Moses wrote, "Fix these words of mine in your hearts and minds. . . . Teach them to your children, talking about them when you sit at home and when you walk along the road, when you lie down and when you get up. Write them on the doorframes of your houses and on your gates, so that your days and the days of your children may be many in the land that the Lord swore to give your forefathers."

The Israelites understood that the transferring of their faith would not occur in a single event, like a baby dedication, but was a continual, lifelong discipline. They were not to assume that their children would embrace their values. Instead, they were to make a deliberate effort to saturate their youth with God's Word.

In the New Testament, Paul wrote to a young minister named Timothy: "I have been reminded of your sincere faith, which first lived in your grandmother Lois and in your mother Eunice and, I am persuaded, now lives in you also" (2 Timothy 1:5).

Throughout Scripture we are instructed to teach the next generation to know the Word of God and to walk in his will. It is not just the responsibility of parents, but also of grandparents, aunts, uncles, teachers, coaches, youth sponsors, scout leaders, ministers, and all Christian adults to influence the next generation for Christ:

"The things you have heard me say in the presence of many witnesses entrust to reliable men who will also be qualified to teach others" (2 Timothy 2:2).

"Teach the older women to . . . train the younger women to love their husbands and children" (Titus 2:3-4).

Some of those studied in this book were parents, and some were just significant adults who impacted young people. So, while these studies will have an obvious application to parents and grandparents, I hope they will have meaning for any adult who cares about the future of the church and the nation.

"Find Us Faithful"

We're pilgrims on the journey of the narrow road,
And those who've gone before us line the way.
Cheering on the faithful, encouraging the weary,
Their lives a stirring testament to God's sustaining grace.

Surrounded by so great a cloud of witnesses,
Let us run the race not only for the prize;
But as those who've gone before us,
Let us leave to those behind us
The heritage of faithfulness passed on through Godly lives.

After all our hopes and dreams have come and gone,
And our children sift through all we've left behind,
May the clues that they discover
And the memories they uncover
Become the light that leads them to the road we each must find.

O may all who come behind us find us faithful,
May the fire of our devotion light their way.
May the footprints that we leave lead them to believe
And the lives we live inspire them to obey.
O may all who come behind us find us faithful.

CHAPTER ONE

Demonstrate Priorities

Abraham and Isaac

Genesis 22:1-14

Pianist Roger Williams spoke of being the son of a preacher. He said when he was a child that one of his playmates boasted, "My dad is a doctor, and I can get sick for nothing."

Another of Williams' friends said, "My dad is a pilot, and I can fly for nothing."

Williams said, "My dad is a preacher, and I can be good for nothing!"

I've often wondered why so many preachers' kids turn out to be rebellious. Not all of them do, of course. Some of the finest Christians I've known have been the children of ministers. But some of the wildest people I have known—and a disproportionate number, it seems—grew up in the homes of preachers, too.

Sometimes, it is the child's fault. When someone passes the baton, it can be passed perfectly and the next runner can drop it. The giver and the receiver both have responsibility.

But there is one trait that I have consistently observed in the lives of ministers who have successfully passed the baton of faith on to their children: authenticity. When the person in the pulpit is the same person in the parsonage, his children don't see their parent as a phony. They can be confident that God genuinely comes first in his life.

Howard Hendricks, a professor at Dallas Theological Seminary, is a popular Christian speaker on family values. Many years ago I heard him tell of a conversation he had with his two grown children. His daughter said, "Dad, I've often wondered why we never resented you being gone so much when we were children. You traveled a lot, speaking and preaching, but we never were bitter about that the way some kids were."

Hendricks's son said, "Bev, don't you think it is because of Mom and her attitude? She never griped about Dad's preaching schedule."

His son continued: "She never said, 'Good night, he's gone again! He's lecturing to others, but he neglects his own. The church gets him more than we do.' On the contrary, the memories I have are of taking Dad to the airport and waving goodbye, then going home and praying for his trip. Mom would tell us how blessed we were to have a father that other people wanted to hear. Then we would go back and pick Dad up at the airport, and listen to his report."

Hendricks said, "To this day, my children ask for my preaching schedule so they can pray for my ministry. They are faithful to the Lord, and I attribute that to the attitude of their mother, who was always positive and supportive."

For us to transfer the baton of faith to the next generation, others must sense that obedience to God is the first priority in our lives. Hendricks and his wife shared that commitment, and together they passed on the baton of faith to their children by putting God first in their lives.

The story of Abraham and Isaac provides an excellent example of a father demonstrating priorities, and passing the baton of faith to the next generation.

God Comes First

"God said, '[Abraham,] take your son, your only son, Isaac, whom you love, and go to the region of Moriah. Sacrifice him there as a burnt offering'" (Genesis 22:2).

Abraham must have been stunned. Pagan nations practiced human sacrifice, but Abraham believed in a loving and just God. Besides, God had promised that Isaac would father many nations. How could that be fulfilled if he were dead?

Isaac was Abraham's only son by his beloved wife Sarah, and they had waited years for this child. He loved Isaac. I'm sure they hunted and fished together, and they certainly worked and worshiped together. Abraham could not imagine killing his son on an altar as he would an animal.

But God came first, so Abraham put his trust in God and made plans to obey. He and Isaac said good-bye to Sarah and headed toward Moriah as God had commanded. They took two servants to assist them, and they traveled for three days until they reached the base of the mountain.

> He said to his servants, "Stay here with the donkey while I and the boy go over there. We will worship and then we will come back to you" (Genesis 22:5).

It is interesting that Abraham said, "WE will come back to you." Though he had been commanded to take the life of Isaac, somehow Abraham believed that God would still keep his promise to make Isaac the father of many nations. Hebrews 11:19 says, "Abraham reasoned that God could raise the dead." Abraham knew that if God could give him a son when he was 100 years old, he could certainly raise that son back from the dead.

Still, Abraham had to have been heartsick as he climbed that mountain with his son.

> Isaac spoke up and said to his father Abraham, "Father?"
> "Yes, my son?" Abraham replied.
> "The fire and the wood are here," Isaac said, "But where is the lamb for the burnt offering?" (Genesis 22:7).

Isaac knew all about worship. They had done this before. I am sure Abraham had to choke back the tears when he heard Isaac's perceptive but innocent question.

> Abraham answered, "God himself will provide the lamb for the burnt offering, my son." And the two of them went on together (Genesis 22:8).

When they reached the top of the mountain, Abraham began to build a makeshift altar. I think he then turned to Isaac and began to explain God's command. Isaac, a prototype of Jesus, was apparently willing to do what his father instructed, allowing himself to be bound without resistance. Abraham laid his son on the altar and raised the knife to kill him.

Suddenly an angel of God interrupted.

> "Abraham! Abraham!"
>
> "Here I am," he replied.
>
> "Do not lay a hand on the boy," he said. "Do not do anything to him. Now I know that you fear God, because you have not withheld from me your son, your only son" (Genesis 22:11, 12).

Abraham looked and saw a ram caught by its horns in the thicket. He quickly and joyfully untied Isaac. Then he took the ram and offered it as a sacrifice in the place of his son. In gratitude for the Lord's provision of the ram, Abraham gave the place a new name. He called it, "The Lord Will Provide" (Genesis 22:14). Then the two of them, father and son, headed down the mountain and toward home.

Children Must Know God Is First in Our Lives

There was one message that Isaac learned that day: Abraham's faith in God was the foremost priority in his life. Isaac knew that he was loved, but on that day Abraham demonstrated that he loved God even more than he loved Isaac.

Perhaps that is the reason Isaac didn't rebel against his father's faith. He didn't say, "My dad's fanatic religion nearly cost me my life! I want nothing to do with God; I don't want to put my children through what I've been through." Isaac embraced his father's faith because he saw that it was, without question, the most important factor in his life.

In Hebrews 11, Abraham is listed as one of the great Old Testament heroes of the faith. After documenting Abraham's faith, the writer adds, "By faith Isaac blessed Jacob and Esau in regard to their future" (Hebrews 11:20). Abraham had successfully passed the baton of faith to his son.

Until young people sense that obedience to God is first in our lives, they will probably object to all of our lecturing and sermonizing, and in turn, they will reject our values. Here are some practical ways we can authentically demonstrate to young people that God comes first in our lives:

Priorities Are Demonstrated by Our Attitude Toward the Church

When I was growing up, my family never missed church. On Sunday morning, Sunday night, and Wednesday night, we never asked, "Are we going to church?" It was just, "What time are we leaving?" Only once did I ever ask my parents if I could stay home from church, and I discovered quickly that it was foolish even to ask.

If parents want to eliminate the hassle of children complaining about going to church, they can do so by settling the issue early in the child's life. Communicate to the child that it is not a matter for discussion.

Some parents will say, "I don't want to force religion on my children. I'm afraid it will turn them off later." But we force our children to take showers, to eat their vegetables, to take their medicine, and to go to school. If we don't make them go to church, we send the message that going to school and learning about science is important, but going to church and learning about God is an option. For every person you find who complains that he doesn't go to church because his parents made him go when he was younger, I'll find you twenty people who claim they do go to church because their parents made them go when they were younger!

I have an indelible memory of an event that occurred when I was nine years old. I had come home from a Little League baseball practice as excited as I could be about my first chance to go to a major league baseball game. I said, "Mom and Dad, our baseball team is going to go to Cleveland to see the Indians play baseball!" I had always wanted to see a major league game. "All we have to do," I said, "is wear our Little League uniforms and we get in free. We're supposed to take a sack lunch and ride a bus, and we get to see the Indians play!"

My parents were excited, too, until they checked the date and said, "Bob, that's a Sunday. We go to church. You can't go."

I said, "Oh, just this once, can't I go? I always go to church."

They said, "No. You can't go."

I said, "What am I going to tell my friends?"

They said, "Tell them that they should be in church, too, and if everyone went to church, they'd have to take you to the ball game on another day."

(Oh, sure, that's what I was going to tell them!)

That Sunday we went to church and drove right by the kids in Harmonsburg getting on the bus to go to Cleveland. My dad beeped the horn and waved! I dived down into the seat to hide.

A few years later, I did occasionally play in Little League games on Wednesday nights. My parents had finally relented and allowed me to play on Wednesday nights because they reasoned that the Bible didn't command us to worship on Wednesday nights. Even so, those Wednesday night games were the only ones my family didn't come to see. They all went to church.

When I was twelve years old, I pitched in an all-star game on a Wednesday night. That particular game started early enough that my family was able to be there. My team won. Afterwards, our assistant coach, Mr. Nieman, said he was treating everyone to milk shakes at Hank's Frozen Custard. I really wanted to go, but I looked across the parking lot and saw my family hurrying to the car. I knew they were going to church. Suddenly I was faced with a decision.

I said, "Coach, I'm not going to Hank's. I'm going with my parents." I ran across the parking lot calling, "Wait for me!" and I went to church in my baseball uniform.

I never had to question what came first in the lives of my parents. They communicated their priorities by demonstration. I knew that the Lord was even more important to them than their son.

In contrast, I know of a Christian family that missed church every weekend during the fall when their son was playing college football. They traveled every weekend to see their son play football on Saturday; then they drove home on Sunday. They said, "We hate to miss church, but we think it's important that our son knows we support him. We think the Lord understands." But the tragic message that was communicated to that son was that he was more important to his parents than God was.

God wants us to love and support our children, but he commands us to honor him above all others. Usually we can do both if we will use some creativity.

Every fall, the Dabney family of our church has a weekend get-together in Gatlinburg, Tennessee. Though many families would use such a weekend retreat as an excuse to skip church, the Dabneys do not. On Sunday morning they have their own worship service in their cabin. Someone leads singing, another person serves Communion, and someone else delivers a sermon.

One year they even produced a bulletin for the service. The front of the bulletin read, "The First Primitive Weekend Getaway Christian Church on the Hill." Inside was the order of worship, listing all of the participants in the service. The bulletin noted that their offering would be donated to a crisis-pregnancy center in Louisville, Kentucky. (They collected seventy-one dollars for the center.) It even included announcements and a "thank you" to the grandparents for providing the weekend and for their ever-growing love.

Those are the kinds of things that create memories and, more importantly, communicate priorities. Even when we are on vacation, God should come first. David said in Psalm 122:1, "I rejoiced with those who said to me, 'Let us go to the house of the Lord.'"

But what about parents whose older children aren't accustomed to attending church regularly? Maybe the parents were converted later in life, or maybe they have just been permissive and not required that the children attend church regularly. Should they now begin demanding that the children attend church?

The goal is to win the child's heart, not to force correct behavior. Therefore, parents should be careful in applying their new understanding to the child's life. It might not be wise to require that he attend church Sunday morning, Sunday night and Wednesday night, and that he attend all youth functions, if that is a complete reversal for him. Such demands might sour his attitude about church. Perhaps the parents can require one additional step of commitment for their child, and then stick to that commitment.

Wayne Smith, minister of the Southland Christian Church in Lexington, Kentucky, told me, "Everyone has a saturation point. My wife and I attend all three worship services on Sunday morning, and then we go to church on Sunday night. I come home after church on Sunday night, and my wife is watching Charles Stanley on TV! That's fanatical!" He said, "After I've been to church four times, I don't want to watch Charles Stanley on TV. I want to watch Clint Eastwood!"

Parents must be sensitive to the spiritual level of their children, and bring them along wisely. However, they need to recognize that children are going to complain and beg to stay home. They'll find something more exciting, regardless of how effective the church program is. That is human nature. There should still be some requirements—at least a commitment to weekly corporate worship—so that the children know the parents' priorities. The parents must communicate as early as possible what those requirements are, and then be committed to them.

We must also remember that communicating our attitude toward the church is deeper than simply attending regularly. When our children observe our behavior in worship, do they see us involved or passive? Do they sense that we are being supportive of the church leaders or critical? Do they sense an appreciation for the body of Christ or a pride in our independence? If we complain all the way home about the music, the sermon, or how long the service lasted, then we are telling our children that church is a source of irritation instead of a celebration.

Our church recently made a large three-year commitment for a new building program. I was very proud of our church's response, and I was especially proud of our teenagers. Our sixth- through twelfth-graders who attend our teen worship service committed to give over $71,000.00 in the next three years to our building program. That communicates a lot about our youth leaders, but it communicates even more about the parents of those teenagers. When we get serious about our faith, our young people are going to follow!

Priorities Are Demonstrated by the Atmosphere Created in the Home

> These commandments that I give you today are to be upon your hearts. Impress them on your children. Talk about them when you sit at home and when you walk along the road, when you lie down and when you get up. Tie them as symbols on your hands and bind them on your foreheads. Write them on the doorframes of your houses and on your gates (Deuteronomy 6:6-9).

Our faith is not to be reserved for church only. It should spill over and impact every area of our lives, particularly in our homes.

John Foster, the chairman of our board, has two plaques on the posts outside his front door. One of them reads, "Foster home, established 1954." The other reads, "As for me and my house, we will serve the Lord."

I distinctly remember the words of a plaque that hung in the kitchen of my parents' home: "Jesus Christ is the head of this house, the unseen guest at every meal, the silent listener to every conversation."

Christians are wise to hang pictures of Christ and Scripture verses on the walls of their homes. There should be Christian magazines in our magazine racks, and Christian books and videos on our shelves. It is good for children of all ages to have access to Christian music. Saying grace before meals and conversations about God should be a natural part of a Christian's home.

Some might say we are getting too fanatical about our faith, but they're the same people that you will see with T-shirts, bumper stickers, wastebaskets, and ball caps that declare their loyalty to their favorite sports teams. If they can be sports fans, then we can be faith fans!

Parents sing *Sesame Street* songs with their kids, or songs that Barney, the big purple dinosaur, sings. Shouldn't our children also hear us sing songs like "Jesus Loves Me" and other choruses about our faith?

The atmosphere in your home demonstrates what is really important in your life. Is the Bible visible? Is it ever read? Do your children ever hear you pray for them?

I heard one man say, "I heard my mother pray for me every day. She would always say, 'May God help you if you ever do that again!'"

When our first son was only a few months old, we began to have devotions every night before bed. We would read a Bible story book, *The Bible in Pictures for Little Eyes.* Then we would join hands and have prayer. As our sons grew older, the Bible stories matured as well. Eventually, we simply read a passage of Scripture and then joined hands and had prayer. They may seem like little things, but they make big impressions. We were reminded daily of who the final authority was in our home.

Our boys are grown and gone now, but every night before my wife and I go to sleep, we still join hands and have prayer together.

Priorities Are Demonstrated by Adherence to God's Commands

We most effectively demonstrate to others that our faith comes first when we ourselves adhere to God's commands. Children are keenly aware of our behavior. We may not realize it, but children carefully watch us to see if our walk matches our talk.

Years ago, on New Year's Day, my wife answered the phone and I heard her say, "Sure, come on over and see us! We'd love to have you!" She hung up and told me that a certain family from our church who had recently moved out of town was back visiting and was stopping by to see us.

I said, "Oh, no! I wanted to just relax, watch football, and be with the family today. I've kind of had it up to here with people . . . and that woman is a talker! They'll be here for hours!"

They came, and we had a great visit together. They only stayed about forty-five minutes because they had somewhere else they had to go. We had a wonderful time fellowshiping with them, so, as they were leaving, I said, "Hey, thanks for coming by! We really enjoyed having you!"

As I shut the door, my son, Rusty, who was about ten years old at the time, said, "Dad, you hypocrite!"

I said, "What do you mean?"

He said, "You said you didn't want them to come, and then you told them you were glad they came."

I tried feebly to explain that I had changed my mind. But the issue made me keenly aware of how carefully young people scrutinize our behavior.

Your children are listening when you answer the phone and say, "Sorry, he's not here," when he really is.

They're listening when you sit at the table and talk about the woman at work who is having an affair with the supervisor, and they hear you laugh.

They're listening when you make a racial slur against the neighbor who irritates you.

They're observing your intake of alcohol and how it affects you.

They notice whether you treat their mother or their father with thoughtfulness or neglect.

They're learning when you help them with their homework, and then finally say, "Just let me do it for you."

They see how upset you become when you're cheated out of money or one of your favorite possessions is damaged.

They observe the kind of television programs and videos you watch.

They hear you say, "You know, your education is the most important thing in your life."

Who you are makes a far greater impact on children than could ever be counteracted by an hour of Sunday school or church, or even a few minutes of a devotion at the end of a day.

Paul Ryden, who now works as a feature reporter in Atlanta, once lived in Louisville and was a member of our church. He had not been a Christian for very long when he was asked to speak to a junior-high class about being a Christian in the media. He did a great job, and the kids fell in love with him. Several nights later, he was climbing the steps of Freedom Hall at halftime of a University of Louisville basketball game. He had a beer in his hand and just happened to pass some of the teens who had been in that class. They stopped, exchanged greetings, laughed and talked for a few moments, but when he sat down, he suddenly felt uncomfortable with that beer. He thought to himself, "Maybe I can handle this beer, but maybe they can't. And this is probably not the image I want to convey if I am going to influence junior-high young people." At that moment, he decided to become a total abstainer. He decided that his influence on the next generation was more important than his personal freedom.

Sports Illustrated reported on a T-ball game in Wellington, Florida, where a seven-year-old first baseman, Tanner Munsey, fielded a ground ball and tried to tag a runner going from first to second. The umpire, Laura Benson, called the runner out. But young Tanner immediately went to the umpire and said, "Ma'am, I didn't touch him." The umpire reversed her decision and sent the runner back to second base. Tanner's coach awarded him the game ball for his honesty.

Two weeks later, Laura Benson was again the umpire, and Tanner Munsey was playing shortstop when a similar play occurred. This time, Benson ruled that Tanner had missed the tag on the runner going to third base, and she called the runner safe. Tanner, with a strange expression, but without saying a word, tossed the ball to the pitcher and returned to his position. Benson, sensing that Tanner was troubled, asked Tanner, "Did you tag the runner?" He said, "Yes." Benson called the runner out!

The opposing coach came roaring onto the field to protest, but Laura Benson explained to him what had happened two weeks earlier.

"If a kid is that honest," she said, "I have to give it to him. This game is supposed to be for kids"[1]

If you had been that coach, would you have given Tanner Munsey the game ball? If you had been the opposing coach, would you have remembered that the game is for kids? If you had been the umpire, would you have encouraged that kind of integrity? If you had been Tanner's parents, would you have been proud of him?

Congratulations, Tanner Munsey! Congratulations, parents! Congratulations, coach! Congratulations, Laura Benson!

May those who come behind us find us as faithful.

[1] *Sports Illustrated,* "Bits and Pieces," September 16, 1993.

CHAPTER TWO

Communicate Love

Jacob and His Sons

Genesis 37:1-10

S ince my youth, O God, you have taught me, and to this day I declare your marvelous deeds. Even when I am old and gray, do not forsake me, O God, till I declare your power to the *next generation*, your might to *all who are to come* (Psalm 71:17, 18, emphasis mine).

In an advertisement for one of our local banks, a mother is shown putting her first-grader on the bus and waving good-bye. "Every morning, we send our children one day closer to the future," the announcer says. More dramatic footage of young children follows, with the announcer concluding, "The best investment in the future is an investment in our children."

The advertisers are right, except that our primary concern should not be financial investments but spiritual investments. Christians should be very concerned about investing in the spiritual future of our children. We should deposit in our youth a rich faith in God and leave them an inheritance of biblical values so they will be protected against the propaganda with which Satan is saturating their minds.

Though we usually like to learn by imitating the positive examples of others, we can often learn from the mistakes of others how not to handle certain responsibilities. Such is the case with Jacob, one of my least favorite Bible characters.

When I get to Heaven, Jacob is not going to be first on my list of people to meet. Too much of what we know of Jacob is negative. He was a deceiver as a young man, tricking his own father into believing he was his older brother Esau (Genesis 27:1-37). He had two wives and two concubines, an obvious breach of God's intention for one man to be faithful to one wife for life. As a father, he failed to set a consistent example of faith and leadership, openly favoring some of his children (first Joseph and then Benjamin) over the others. As a result, even though he believed in God and took his faith seriously, he had a difficult time passing along his values to his twelve sons.

This does not negate the good that he did. Jacob took a stand for the Lord when he ordered his household (which included servants as well as family) to "get rid of the foreign gods you have with you, and purify yourselves" (Genesis 35:2). In spite of his errors as a father, he did instill in his son Joseph a strong moral character that enabled him to remain faithful to God in spite of being sold into slavery, falsely accused of evil, and thrown into prison. Jacob himself is listed with the faithful in Hebrews 11, as is his son Joseph.

Still, Jacob's example is usually a negative one. By studying his errors, we can learn the importance of communicating love to our children.

A Snapshot of a Dysfunctional Home

The story of Jacob's family reads like a soap opera. The events leading up to the birth of his son Joseph reveal the shaky underpinnings of this dysfunctional home. Jacob was in love with his wife Rachel, but she was childless. Rachel lived in self-pity while she was forced to watch Jacob father ten children by three other women.

After several years, Rachel finally gave birth to a son, Joseph, and both parents were elated. But even after the birth of Joseph, Jacob continued to make some big mistakes as a father that we should learn to avoid.

For one, Jacob made no attempt to conceal which of his sons was his favorite.

Now Israel [Jacob's God-given name] loved Joseph more than any of his other sons, because he had been born to him in his old age; and he made a richly ornamented robe for him. When his brothers saw that their father loved him more than any of them, they hated him and could not speak a kind word to him (Genesis 37:3, 4).

This was no typical sibling rivalry. This was bitter hatred that turned to violence and ripped Jacob's home apart.

Joseph further alienated his brothers when he told them about one of his dreams.

> He said to them, "Listen to this dream I had: We were binding sheaves of grain out in the field when suddenly my sheaf rose and stood upright, while your sheaves gathered around mine and bowed down to it."
>
> His brothers said to him, "Do you intend to reign over us? Will you actually rule us?'" And they hated him all the more because of his dream and what he had said (Genesis 37:6-8).

Joseph's brothers hated him so much that they plotted to kill him—their own brother! But at the last minute, they changed their minds and sold him to some passing slave traders. Then, to deceive their father, they took that special coat of Joseph's, soaked it with blood, and told Jacob that his favorite son must have been torn apart by a wild beast.

Though Jacob was beside himself with grief and refused to be comforted, Jacob's sons lived with that lie for twenty-two years. When they later discovered that Joseph was still alive, their hearts seemed to be somewhat softer, but the family record during those twenty-two years includes rape, incest, immorality, bitterness, and murder. Jacob had made some terrible mistakes in his efforts to pass his faith on to his children.

There are two obvious mistakes that Jacob made:

Jacob Did Not Communicate Unconditional Love to All of His Children

There was nothing wrong with Jacob's loving Joseph and giving him a special coat. Children need positive strokes, and they need the security of knowing that someone thinks they're special. My wife was always calling our two sons her "favorite." She would say, "You're my favorite younger son," or "You're my favorite older son." She once told one of my sons who had just sat the bench for an entire basketball game, "You're my favorite basketball player on the bench!"

Jacob's mistake was in ignoring his other sons. He doted over Joseph and seemed oblivious to the needs of his other sons.

No wonder they hated Joseph. They were probably starving for attention from their father. That does not excuse their behavior, but it helps us understand it. When we read the rest of their story, we discover that those young men were insecure, insensitive, and unspiritual. Not one brother felt enough compassion for his father to tell him the truth, though Jacob mourned for twenty-two years.

Jacob Failed to Train His Sons to Love Others

Jesus said the first commandment is to love God with all your heart, and the second is to love others as yourself. But the sons of Jacob had no idea how to show love even to their own brothers. They were as self-centered as they could be. If Joseph had been sensitive to the feelings of his brothers, he would not have flaunted his dreams. And the others should have cared enough for Joseph to want to protect him. Instead, they spoke of killing him and then sold him into slavery.

We learn, then, two important lessons from the negative example of Jacob and his family.

Children Need to Know They Are Loved Unconditionally

CBN News recently had a feature about immorality among teenagers. When they interviewed one young woman who was involved in promiscuous behavior, they asked her why she was going to such extremes of sin. She responded, "It is because kids are lonely. If you don't get love at home, you'll go find it someplace else, or with someone else."

School teachers agree. Teachers consistently report that their problem students are primarily those children who are not confident of their parent's love for them. The resulting insecurity is reflected in the student's lack of concentration and lack of discipline.

Gary and Anna Marie Ezzo have developed an excellent child-rearing course, *Growing Kids God's Way*. They suggest that there are five ways to communicate love to others. They call them "languages of love."[1]

The first language of love is *encouraging words*. Paul said in 1 Corinthians 8:1, "Love builds up." We can express love to people simply by giving them verbal encouragement: "You're special," "I need you," "You are thoughtful," "I learn from you," "You look nice," "I love you." All of those phrases—and many other encouraging words—communicate love. We all feel loved when someone takes the time to express it verbally through words of praise and recognition.

Acts of service comprise the second language of love. In 1 John 3:18 we read, "Let us not love with words or tongue but with actions and in truth." We can communicate love to others by doing something special for them that we know will be appreciated—something that goes beyond what is normal or expected.

David Williams plays football for the Houston Oilers. His wife gave birth to their first child the day before the Oilers were to play the New England Patriots. Williams decided he would stay home with his wife rather than play in the game. His decision cost him one week's salary: $111,000! But his act of service was a tangible way he could communicate to his wife that he loved her more than football and more than money.

A third way to express love is through *gift giving*. Ephesians 5:25 says, "Christ loved the church and gave himself up for her." The simple gesture of a thoughtful gift is a great way to express love. An impromptu gift, at a time other than Christmas or a birthday, is especially meaningful because it says, "When we were apart, you were on my mind."

Quality time is a fourth expression of love. Jesus often took his disciples apart from the crowds to a quiet place where they could spend time alone. Quality time means investing yourself in the other person by listening carefully and responding lovingly. It doesn't mean sitting in the same room with someone while you both stare at a television or one of you reads the newspaper. Quality time requires active participation in positive conversation. It means going beyond the surface level of communication.

Physical touch and closeness make up the final language of love. Jesus communicated love by touching the little children, the blind, the deaf, and even the lepers. We communicate love when we hold someone's hand, put an arm around someone's shoulder, or give someone a hug.

According to the Ezzos, every person has a primary language of love—one mode of expression that means more than the other four. It is the love language one most enjoys receiving from someone else and the one he tends to use to express love to others.

It is important in any successful relationship that we learn to speak the same love languages. After studying the Ezzos' five languages of love, I asked my wife to list her love languages in order, with her primary love language at the top of the list and the language that is the least meaningful to her at the bottom. Then I asked her to list what she thought mine would be. I did the same for myself and for her. It was a good experiment. After twenty-eight years of marriage, we both came pretty close to knowing the other's love language preferences. Judy's primary love language is physical touch. Mine is quality time. The one that interests her the least is acts of service. My least favorite is gift giving.

It doesn't take much imagination to see how couples can get into conflict if they are not speaking the same love language. A husband whose primary language of love is physical touch comes home and says, "How about a hug?" But the wife's primary language may be words of encouragement, so she is secretly wishing he would speak poetically to her about how pretty she is or how much he loves her. She knocks herself out to serve him in hopes that he will notice and say, "Thanks for your efforts! You're so special!" Instead, though he may notice, he rarely says much. Words of encouragement may be his least favorite language of love, so he fails to communicate to her in her primary love language. He tries to compensate with physical touch—his primary love language—but she can't understand why he just wants a kiss. And he can't understand why his attempts to communicate love seem to be missing the mark.

Gary Ezzo writes, "We must not only learn to speak the primary love language of our partner, but also to receive graciously all the expressions of love that come our way from those around us."[2]

Children, too, need to hear their primary language of love spoken. If it can be that difficult to communicate with our spouses in their language of love, it is very important that we study our children to discover what their primary love languages might be and learn to communicate to them in those languages.

My son Phil says "I love you" with gifts. He loves to buy big gifts. A couple of years ago I played in the local Foster Brooks Golf Tournament. Just before the tournament, Phil bought a very nice golf bag for me. My name was printed on it in bold letters as if I were a pro golfer! I was a little embarrassed because having my name stamped on my golf bag was not really my style. Besides, the way I play, I don't usually want people to know who I am! But it was a great way for Phil to say, "I care." At the time, I didn't react as excitedly as I wish I had. Gift giving is last on my list of love languages and first on his, and I have had to learn to communicate in his love language.

One couple told of coming home from a weekend trip and bringing a teddy bear for each of their two daughters. They said, "When we gave one to Jennifer, she said excitedly, 'Mom, Dad, thank you! This is wonderful! I love this teddy bear.'" As she hugged and kissed them, the parents thought, "What a thankful heart."

When they gave their younger daughter Amy her gift, she replied, "Thanks. This is nice. Can we talk for a while?"

The parents pleaded, "Amy, don't you like your new teddy bear?"

Amy said, "Yes, I like it, but let's talk for a few minutes."

After trying to convince her how wonderful the gift was, the parents concluded that Amy must not be as thankful as Jennifer.

That was the wrong conclusion. Amy may have been just as grateful, but they didn't understand the love languages of their two daughters. One daughter's love language was gift giving. The other's was quality time.

The parents admitted that when they began to understand those differences, it was much easier to communicate love to both girls. They would often come home and Jennifer would say, "I made you a surprise!" She had usually baked something as her act of love. In return, they would do the same for her. Even a small gift like a ribbon for her hair would brighten her face. They were speaking her love language.

Since quality time was Amy's love language, they would take her out for a leisurely lunch. Though Jennifer enjoyed such lunches, they discovered that quality time meant much more to Amy. By giving her their undivided attention, she felt they were saying "I love you" in a language she could understand.[3]

As our children are growing up, we should pay careful attention to see which love language is becoming their primary language. Gary Ezzo wrote,

> It is difficult to distinguish a primary love language in a child before age seven. All children under seven like presents, hugs and quality time. By age seven, however, the primary love language of a child has developed sufficiently to be recognized.

The primary love language will be the one the child uses most often to communicate love to others, and the language he most wants others to express to him.

Proverbs 22:6 says, "Train up a child in the way he should go, and when he is old he will not turn from it." When parents or other adults fail to understand a child's primary love language, the adults get frustrated, and the child can become confused and uncertain of their love. But an understanding of this principle will help adults communicate to children that they are loved and appreciated.

Children Need to Be Taught to Love Others

Paul wrote, "Do nothing out of selfish ambition or vain conceit, but in humility consider others better than yourselves. Each of you should look not only to your own interests, but also to the interests of others" (Philippians 2:3, 4).

Jacob not only failed to communicate unconditional love to all of his sons, he also failed to teach his sons how to love other people. His sons did not care for the welfare of each other or that of their father.

Young people need to know that they are loved unconditionally, but they also need to be taught that they are not living in isolation. They are not the only ones who are loved. There are other people living in this world who are just as valuable to God as they are, and those people deserve to be treated with respect and kindness. The Ezzos call it, "Valuing the preciousness of others."

There was an excellent editorial in our local newspaper recently, entitled, "A Generation of Free Agents." In it, Cheryl Russell gets to the heart of what happens when people fail to value others, putting their own needs first in every situation. She writes:

Something is going wrong in the U.S. Our public schools are failing. Our citizens are apathetic. Poverty rates are rising. Health care costs are soaring. Businesses are going under by the thousands. The list of ills is a long one. But why? No one has been able to fully explain why things seem to have taken such a turn for the worse. Everyone can cite what is wrong—divorce, crime, drug abuse, obsessive materialism, lack of duty and commitment and an unwillingness to sacrifice for the public good. Everyone also seems to know when things started to unravel—about three decades ago. Newsweek calls our recent history, "The 30 year spree."

The core reason for the upheaval in American society lies in the maturation of the enormous baby boom generation. It's more than a coincidence that America's social fabric began to tear just as the baby boom generation, born between 1946 and 1964, came of age in the late sixties.

Boomers' attitudes and values are profoundly different from those of older Americans. At the root of these differences is a strong sense of individualism instilled in baby boomers by their parents. Baby boomers' parents reared their children to think for and of themselves.

Studies of child-rearing practices show that parents of the 1950's and 1960's consistently ranked, "To think for themselves" as the number one trait they wanted to nurture in their children.

Post-war affluence also allowed parents to indulge their children as never before.

Now some social observers decry this individualism. They blame young people for selfishness and demand Americans show more concern for community needs. But the individualistic perspective is not something baby boomers can turn on and off like a faucet. It's not a simple choice, such as buying a new pair of jeans. It is not even a conscious pursuit. Instead, it is the way these men and women see and relate to the world. . . . It is the ma⸳· ⁻ trend of their time. It is behind the rise in divorce and violent crime. ιt ιs the reason for soaring health care costs, political gridlock and racial tensions.

. . . Individualists put their personal needs ahead of community needs. They make commitments for personal gain rather than moral reasons. . . . In essence, the baby boomer is the first American generation of "free agents."[4]

But individualism is nothing new. It dates all the way back to the Garden of Eden when Satan persuaded Adam and Eve to disregard God's instructions and think for themselves. The Bible calls it selfishness, pride, and sin.

Our primary goal as parents and adult leaders is not to rear young people to think for themselves. The Bible tells us that man in his wisdom does not know God, and that the wisdom of man is foolishness with God. Our goal is to rear young people who have the mind of Christ. They are not to be free agents, but God's servants. It should not be the "me" generation, but the "we" generation. We want young people who know how to love others, who know they are loved by others and by God. We need young people who put the needs of others ahead of their own.

Paul continues in Philippians 2, "Your attitude should be the same as that of Christ Jesus, who . . . humbled himself and became obedient to death, even death on a cross!" (Philippians 2:5-8).

That is counterculture, but it is what we are instructed by God to do. Unselfish behavior is what produces a lasting society and more fulfilled individuals.

Let's consider some practical ways to instill an attitude of unselfishness in others.

A little child is running through the fellowship hall of the church during a crowded activity. The parents say to the child, "Stop running." That may temporarily restrain the child's behavior, but it does not teach the child why running in a crowded room is not appropriate behavior.

The child needs to know that other people are to be loved and respected, and to run in a crowded room is not being respectful of others. Older people who are not very stable might be frightened or even knocked down. Parents of little babies will be concerned that something might happen to their little ones if a child is running nearby. One child's running might influence others to do the same, and someone might get hurt.

"It is not enough to teach your children how to *act* morally," says Ezzo. "They must learn to *think* morally."[5]

If your child tosses a candy wrapper at a wastebasket and misses, how do you respond? Do you bend down and pick it up for him? Do you let it lie? Do you shout at your child to pick up the wrapper?

The child needs to be taught why throwing a candy wrapper on the floor is selfish. Someone—a janitor, or perhaps the child's mother, will eventually have to pick up that wrapper. One who values the preciousness of others will pick it up and throw it away so that someone else is not inconvenienced.

That is the reason we should take care of our environment. Christians should not get caught up in the pantheistic philosophy that claims all of nature is God and therefore is sacred. (God has made a distinction between plants, animals, and man, and he has given us dominion over the earth.) But Christians should not be unconcerned about the environment, either. We have an even better reason not to litter the highways or pollute the streams: we care about others. We don't throw a banana peel on the street, even if it is biodegradable and will rot later because we don't want to inconvenience others. We want others to enjoy the beauty of the roadside scenery without the stain of garbage. We want others to be able to fish in the streams and breathe the air. We protect our environment for the benefit of those who come behind us.

Here is another application of the same principle. The signs in the parking lot of a supermarket ask us to return our grocery carts to the designated areas. But who has not seen grocery carts in the ditches, in the middle of parking places and all over the lot? If we value the preciousness of others, we are not going to leave a shopping cart squeezed between two cars.

Jesus said we are to do unto others as we would have them do unto us. How do you like it when you return to your car and find two carts pushed up against it, possibly scratching the car and causing a nuisance for you? How do you feel when you pull into a lot and discover that the parking place closest to the door has three shopping carts parked there? If you leave your shopping cart in an inconvenient place, you create those feelings in others.

We should teach our children how to think of others even in the smallest of situations.

You may say to your child, "Don't talk during church." But does the child know why? You might say, "This is God's house." But God listens to others when they talk out loud. You don't talk in church because it is distracting for others who are trying to listen to the service.

Every mother knows how irritating it can be when her preschooler comes to her while she is involved in a conversation and says, "Mommy, mommy, mommy."

Mom says, "Sh-h. Don't interrupt." But does the child ever learn why it is wrong to interrupt? Interrupting is disrespectful to the other person. What she has to say is important, too.

Teaching a child to be sensitive to the feelings and needs of others is teaching him a much greater act of godliness than simply getting him to restrain improper behavior. We want to teach the child how to show love to others, a guiding principle that will help him for a lifetime.

Gary Ezzo tells about his daughter Jennifer returning home from school and joyfully sharing about how badly her team was defeated in kickball. Being joyful over losing seems un-American! But Jennifer's joy was an unselfish joy. During her gym period, she was selected as the team captain. As they began to choose sides for kickball, Jennifer realized that some of her classmates had never been chosen first. In fact, those who were the worst athletes in the class were always chosen last. So Jennifer made a decision. When the other captain picked first and selected Dennis, the best player, Jennifer said, "I'll pick Dori." (Dori was the worst player in the class). The kids were stunned, but the other captain picked the next-best player and Jennifer went up the ladder from the bottom, picking the second-worst player, then the third-worst, and so on.

She said, "Dad, it was great! We got so clobbered! We took the field first and didn't even get our turn to kick!" But by giving those non-athletes the thrill of being chosen first, Jennifer had experienced the joy that comes from valuing the preciousness of others.[6]

Children by nature can be the cruelest members of society. But children who have learned to value others can be used by God to love those who seldom feel loved.

My parents have always been great examples to me of how to value the preciousness of others. They are very unselfish people. I thought of my parents when I heard Harvey Bream say it wasn't until he was out of college that he realized his mother's favorite piece of chicken was not the neck.

Several years ago we met at my sister's house for Thanksgiving. My sister had written us a letter, explaining that their new home did not have much space in the driveway and that parking on the street was not allowed. If the driveway was filled when we arrived, we were to park in the grade school a half mile down the street.

I arrived with my family at 11:00 A.M. and no one was in the drive. I assumed we must have been the first to arrive, and I pulled into the driveway, thankful that I didn't have to walk from the grade school. When we walked inside, there sat my parents, who were in their early seventies at the time. I said, "Where's your car?"

They said, "Oh, we parked down at the grade school so the ones who came later wouldn't have to walk."

I got back in my car and drove down to the school lot. Don't people like that make you sick? No, people like that make life more pleasant for everyone. People like that have the attitude of Christ.

The New Testament tells us repeatedly to think of "one another." Love one another (Romans 13:8), don't judge one another (Romans 14:13), accept one another (Romans 15:7), instruct one another (Romans 15:14), bear with one another (Ephesians 4:2), forgive one another (Ephesians 4:32), admonish one another (Colossians 3:16), encourage one another (Hebrews 10:25), spur one another on toward love and good deeds (Hebrews 10:24).

There is no better way to show the spirit of Christ than to think more of others than you do of yourself. Jesus said, "The Son of Man did not come to be served, but to serve" (Matthew 20:28).

Jesus expressed his love in all of the love languages. He gave us encouraging words: "As the father loves me, so I love you" (cf. John 15:9). He gave us acts of service—he washed the disciples' feet and healed the sick. He gave us quality time, promising, "Surely, I am with you always, to the very end of the age" (Matthew 28:20). He gave us great examples of physical touch when he touched the children, the blind, the deaf, and the lepers. And he gave us the greatest gift he could give: His own life on the cross.

"God demonstrates his own love for us in this: While we were still sinners, Christ died for us" (Romans 5:8).

Jesus said, "A new command I give you: Love one another. As I have loved you, so you must love one another. By this all men will know that you are my disciples, if you love one another" (John 13:34, 35).

[1]Gary and Anna Marie Ezzo, *Growing Kids God's Way.* Chapter 4, How to Say I Love You. (Excerpts used by permission.)

[2]Ezzo, *Growing Kids God's Way*, p. 72.

[3]Ezzo, *Growing Kids God's Way*, p. 73.

[4]Cheryl Russell, "A Generation of Free Agents," Louisville *Courier Journal*, October 24, 1993.

[5]Ezzo, *Growing Kids God's Way*, p. 38.

[6]Ezzo, *Growing Kids God's Way*, pp. 135, 136.

CHAPTER THREE

Teach Responsibility

Jochebed and Miriam

Exodus 2:1-10

Jochebed was heartsick. Her new baby boy had been condemned to die. Pharaoh was concerned that the expanding Hebrew population might become a threat to his authority, so he had decreed that all the male Hebrew babies must be thrown into the Nile River. Jochebed realized she must do something bold and creative or her baby was doomed.

Jochebed made a tiny boat out of a papyrus basket and pitched it with tar to make it waterproof. She probably tested it repeatedly for its seaworthiness. She then made it as soft and comfortable as possible and placed the child in it, strategically positioning the boat on the edge of the Nile River where Pharaoh's daughter came to bathe. She walked away heartbroken.

But Exodus 2:4 says that the baby's sister, Miriam, "stood at a distance to see what would happen to him."

Jochebed had given Miriam a serious assignment: to watch over the baby and try to intervene at just the right moment. Jochebed must have given her detailed instructions. "Don't take your eye off him. If the basket begins to sink in the water, bring it back to me and we'll try again later. When Pharaoh's daughter comes, stay calm. Act casual and inconspicuous.

"If she retrieves the baby, don't go running up too quickly. Give her some time. Then act as if you just happened to pass by. Remember to act as if you have never seen the child before. You are as surprised as she is. Then, after a few moments, casually suggest, 'Would you like for me to get one of the Hebrew women to nurse the baby for you?'

"If she says yes, come and get me quickly. If she says no...." Jochebed may have done a number of role plays, rehearsing with Miriam how she was to respond to each possible situation. It was a serious responsibility for a young girl who was probably no more than twelve or thirteen years old. But she was very much needed at that crucial time.

We know that with God's guidance, every detail worked out perfectly. Pharaoh's daughter came down to the river to bathe and found the basket.

> She opened it and saw the baby. He was crying, and she felt sorry for him. "This is one of the Hebrew babies," she said.
> Then his sister asked Pharaoh's daughter, "Shall I go and get one of the Hebrew women to nurse the baby for you?"
> "Yes, go," she answered. And the girl went and got the baby's mother (Exodus 2:6-8).

Can you imagine Jochebed's joy? She wiped away the tears and praised God as she scurried down toward the riverbank. Then, trying to restrain her enthusiasm, she probably said to Pharaoh's daughter, "What may I do for you, ma'am? Oh, what have we here? Whose little baby is this? Such a cute child—I'll bet he has beautiful parents."

> Pharaoh's daughter said to her, "Take this baby and nurse him for me, and I will pay you." So the woman took the baby and nursed him. When the child grew older, she took him to Pharaoh's daughter and he became her son. She named him Moses, saying, "I drew him out of the water" (Exodus 2:9, 10).

As Jochebed and Miriam carried the baby Moses back home from the Nile, we can be sure Jochebed did two things: She praised God for answered prayer, and she hugged her daughter Miriam, praising her for carrying out such an important assignment with great success.

If we are to pass our faith on to the next generation, parents and other Christian adults must train children how to handle responsibility. If we expect them to be successful as adults in carrying out life's important assignments, then we must equip them while they are young.

U.S. News and World Report ran an article in July of 1993 titled, "When Cities Give Up Their Streets." The report said that firemen in New York City are now allowing kids to turn on the city's fire hydrants without any repercussions, even though the water pressure becomes dangerously low. In effect, the city has solved its problems by just giving up, and they have turned over control of their fire hydrants to potential troublemakers. One letter to the editor of the *New York Times* said, "This is a dangerous precedent, just asking the citizens of this community to adjust to a higher level of disorder."

Young people who are irresponsible are being tolerated, not confronted. Where once we expected young people to adjust their behavior to conform to safe and productive standards, we are now expected to adjust to them! If they are turning on fire hydrants, we just let them go. Someone else will follow them around to turn the hydrants off.

If kids are bringing guns to school, people think we should put metal detectors at the doors and take their guns, then let them come in.

If high school girls are getting pregnant, we distribute condoms and establish day-cares in the schools for the children of those teenagers.

Some parents are even giving their children extra "mugger money" so they can appease potential attackers they may meet in the school hallways.

Our nation is obsessed with self-centered rights and freedoms. Everyone wants to be able to do his own thing without any self-denial or restraining of egos. As a result, we have witnessed dramatic increases in assaults, robbery, accidents, illiteracy, divorce, and murder. People have surrendered and have released control of our cities and schools to irresponsible human beings. Washington, D.C. Policewoman Bonnie O'Neal said, "If you give the impression that anything goes, sooner or later it will."

If this nation is going to survive, we must begin emphasizing to our children the importance of responsibility. We need for children to become responsible adults in their work, their financial dealings, their behavior, and their spiritual lives.

Work

An important part of rearing children is teaching them how to handle work responsibly. The Old Testament commands, "Six days you shall labor and do all your work" (Exodus 20:9).

Young people in the Bible often had chores to do: Miriam looked after her younger brother; Samuel assisted Eli in the temple; David tended his father's sheep.

When most people lived in rural areas, it was not difficult to teach children the responsibility of work. I grew up on a farm. There we had chores out of necessity; there was simply more to do than our parents could do by themselves. I milked cows, weeded the garden, pitched manure, mowed the grass, and baled hay. Those things were a necessary part of our daily routine. On Saturdays, my mother would get out her "job jar." Before we could do anything else that day, we had to finish two jobs from the job jar.

But today, few families live in an environment where it is necessary that children help around the house. We brought up our two sons in a suburban area where my wife and I could have easily done all the chores ourselves.

John Rosemond, a popular family counselor and author,* said he often asks parents whether they regularly expect their children to perform chores around the home for which they are not paid. Not more than one in ten say yes, even though the overwhelming majority of their own parents would have.

> It means that in the span of one generation, we have managed to misplace a very important tenet of childrearing. Simply stated, it is that children should be *contributing* members of their families.[1]

Chores prepare children for adulthood. They also help children develop a sense of appreciation for the work their parents

---

*John Rosemond is the Director of The Center for Affirmative Parenting in Gastonia, North Carolina. He is a syndicated weekly newspaper columnist and featured Parent Columnist for *Better Homes and Gardens* magazine, as well as *Hemispheres*, the United Airlines in-flight magazine. He is the author of *Parent Power, John Rosemond's Six-point Plan for Raising Happy, Healthy Children, Ending the Homework Hassle, Making the "Terrible Twos" Terrific!*, and *To Spank or Not to Spank* (Andrews & McMeel).

do for them. Chores give a child a sense of security, self-esteem, and family belonging, since they are contributing members of the family rather than parasites living off the family.

Rosemond suggests that when children reach the age of three, while they are still eager to please their parents, they should be allowed to assist in making the bed and setting the dinner table, and they should be taught to pick up their toys before going to bed. That sets the stage for increases in responsibilities as the child grows older. For example, Rosemond advises:

> A four- or five-year-old child should be responsible for keeping his room and bathroom orderly. A six-year-old can be taught to vacuum, starting with his own room. By age seven or eight, the child should be responsible for the daily upkeep of his room and bathroom as well as several chores around the home. Once a week, a child this age should be required to do a major cleaning of his room and bathroom. This should include vacuuming, dusting, changing bath and bed linens, and cleaning the tub, lavatory, and commode.
>
> A nine- to ten-year-old should contribute about forty-five minutes of "chore time" to the family on a daily basis and about two hours on Saturday. It helps to organize the daily routines into three fifteen-minute blocks. The first of these should take place first thing in the morning (straightening room and bathroom and feed the dog); the second, right after school (unload the dishwasher and put everything away); the third, after supper (clear the table, rinse dishes, scrub pots and pans, load the dishwasher, and take out the garbage).[2]

When I was growing up, my mother allowed my brother and me to get by without picking up after ourselves. We convinced her that picking up clothes and making beds were jobs girls should do while we did the "man's work": milking cows, plowing the fields, and baling hay. My mother came to my wife Judy just before we married and said, "I must apologize to you. I did not teach Bobby to pick up after himself, and I am sorry."

Judy was sorry, too! I eventually learned that I should be responsible for myself in those areas, and I do much better now than I did when we were first married. But children would make much better mates if their parents would train them while they are young to accept responsibility for themselves.

Abigail Van Buren said, "If you want your children to keep their feet on the ground, then put some responsibility on their shoulders."

Money

Parents today go to great lengths to purchase everything their children desire. As a result, children have little appreciation for the value of money. They grow up knowing that money buys things they like, but they have little knowledge about earning, saving and spending money. They think money comes from the tooth fairy or the automated teller machine, and they never make the connections between saving and spending.

Christian adults must teach children how to be responsible with money. Children must be taught about tithing, saving, and planning for their own expenditures. We might begin by giving them a small allowance or payment for an extra job around the house. By the time they are in junior high, we can calculate how much money they need for their meals and other expenditures for the week and give them that money as allowance at the beginning of the week. We should tell them, "If you run out and you haven't saved enough money for a meal, then you will have to go without."

It is estimated that while adults are able to purchase only fifteen percent of the things they want, the average parents in America give their children eighty percent of everything they request! Most children have unreal expectations about acquiring material things. They have no concept of self-denial or saving to get something they want. They have an unhealthy attitude toward money and do not know how to handle it responsibly.

In his book, *Getting the Best Out of Your Kids,* John Lehman said that his fourteen-year-old son was responsible for cutting the grass every week. Lehman instructed his son to finish the grass by Thursday each week. If it was not done, they would pay the neighbor boy to do it, and they would pay him out of the son's allowance.

The first time Lehman's son forgot to cut the grass, the neighbor boy was not home. But Lehman's twelve-year-old daughter said she would like to try cutting the grass, and she did a very nice job. The fourteen-year-old son couldn't stand having to pay his little sister to cut the grass, and he never again neglected to do his chore!

Teaching responsible money management to children also includes restricting the purchasing of unreasonable items. Your child may want to buy a $125.00 pair of tennis shoes to wear to school. He may need shoes, but you should say, "I will give you $40.00, the price for a reasonably good pair of shoes. If you want that $125.00 pair, you can earn or save the extra money."

I know of a single mother on a limited income who tells her children every fall before school begins exactly how much money they will be given for school clothes for the year. They then know that if they buy that jacket with the special emblem, they will have to wear last year's clothes or hand-me-downs rather than getting new clothes for school.

Teaching children how to be responsible in the area of money requires parents who are wise enough to practice denial and discipline. It also requires that grandparents and other relatives refrain from being too extravagant. Jesus spoke more about stewardship of our money than he did any other subject. He warned, "A man's life does not consist in the abundance of his possessions" (Luke 12:15).

Behavior

Parents are often frustrated because they are unable to teach their children proper behavior. They can't get them to do their chores; they fight to get them in bed on time; their children bicker with one another; they tell their junior higher not to watch MTV, but he does anyway.

Many parents become so embarrassed and frustrated that they give up. I heard of one mother who became so exasperated when her toddler threw a temper tantrum in a grocery store that she yelled, "You just act like that, but when you get home I'm going to tell your mother!" We'd like to deny that they are even ours sometimes! But if we are going to train our children to be responsible members of society, we must train them to be accountable for their own behavior by putting into practice the leverage that God has given us.

Proverbs 22:15 says, "Folly is bound up in the heart of a child, but the rod of discipline will drive it far from him." The Bible certainly does not advocate child abuse, but it does teach that appropriate spankings will help a child learn that there is authority over him, and that he must be responsible for his own behavior. Don Loni said that his mother had a paddle hanging in the kitchen with an inscription that read, "I need thee every hour."

As children grow older, there are other leverages parents can use to discipline them and teach them responsible behavior.

John Rosemond suggests that we teach our children the "Godfather Principle." In order to make a child accept responsibility for misbehavior of any sort, the child's parents must "make him an offer he can't refuse." Rosemond tells of a family trip to the beach in North Carolina. It was an annual event that he and his wife had come to dread because the four-hour ride with their two children was intolerable. Nothing could stop the continual bickering between them. Then one year, they gave each of the kids five colored pieces of cardboard that they called "tickets." With the tickets came three rules: do not bicker, do not make loud noises, and do not interrupt.

The children were told, "Every time you break a rule, you lose a ticket. . . . If you don't have at least one ticket left when we get to the motel, you won't be allowed in the water for two hours. During that time, you'll sit on the beach under an umbrella and watch the rest of us frolic in the surf."

Rosemond writes:

> By the time we were an hour down the road, they'd each lost four of their five tickets.
>
> The next four hours were the quietest we had ever spent, in or out of a car, with Eric and Amy. They said not a word to each other or to us. They clutched those last tickets to their bosoms and stared out the windows. It was the start of the best family vacation we'd ever had![3]

Spirituality

> Children, obey your parents in the Lord, for this is right. "Honor your father and your mother, . . . that it may go well with you and that you may enjoy long life on the earth." . . .
>
> Fathers, do not exasperate your children; instead, bring them up in the training and instruction of the Lord (Ephesians 6:1-4).

Our goal as Christians is not to develop children who are compliant and dependent upon us. We are not trying to rear kids who make us look good. We are trying to develop people who are servants of Jesus Christ, who depend on him and make him look good.

If we are going to teach children spiritual responsibility, then we must do two things. First, we must *saturate them with God's principles early in their lives.*

Psalm 119:11 says, "I have hidden your word in my heart that I might not sin against you."

Children are not going to be responsible for obeying God's guidelines if they don't know what his Word says. They're not going to learn the Bible at school or by watching television or from Scouts. They're not even going to learn much in one hour of Sunday school each week. Parents must saturate their children with God's Word at home.

> These commandments that I give you today are to be upon your hearts. Impress them on your children. Talk about them when you sit at home and when you walk along the road, when you lie down and when you get up. Tie them as symbols on your hands and bind them on your foreheads. Write them on the doorframes of your houses and on your gates (Deuteronomy 6:6-8).

The second thing we must do to teach our children spiritual responsibility is *teach them the principle of sowing and reaping.* Galatians 6:7 says, "Do not be deceived: God cannot be mocked. A man reaps what he sows."

We must allow our children to suffer the consequences of their own mistakes. Some parents, in a misguided effort to love their children, do everything they can to prevent their children from making any mistakes. They don't want the children to have any painful experiences. When the children do make mistakes, the parents rush in to cover things up for them.

A child who is told when to come to supper doesn't come on time, so his parents warm up his meal in the microwave.

If a child forgets to tie his shoe, a parent ties it for him so he doesn't fall down and skin his knee.

A child gets in trouble at school, and the parents rush in to cover it over.

A junior higher procrastinates on his science project and doesn't finish it, so the parents do it for him the night before.

They tell their teens to wait until marriage to have sex, but just in case, some parents provide "protection" for their kids.

If a teenager gets pregnant, often it is the parents who advocate abortion as the easy way out.

This kind of parenting never allows the children to learn the reality of consequences for personal behavior. Often the pattern continues until something happens that is too big for the parents to cover, and the child is completely unprepared to deal with the consequences.

Let's suppose your nine-year-old son is having a birthday party, and he tells his friends that UK basketball coach Rick Pitino is coming to the party as a special guest. Your son has lied. Every parent is tempted to cover it up, so you call Rick Pitino and say, "My son is such a big fan of yours that he has pretended you are coming to his birthday party. We know you can't come by, but could you make a phone call or just send an autographed picture saying, 'Happy Birthday to my good friend Billy,' or something like that, to save him from embarrassment?"

We rush to the child's defense because we think it is the loving thing to do. But it is actually counterproductive. It prevents the child from learning that sin brings pain. Though he apologizes to you, he should have to face the music. He should be required to call his friends and apologize for lying.

And the discipline should be carried out swiftly. If the consequences are delayed, disobedience is encouraged. Solomon wrote, "When the sentence for a crime is not quickly carried out, the hearts of the people are filled with schemes to do wrong" (Ecclesiastes 8:11).

When a child does something bad, he should feel bad about it. Often it is the parents who end up feeling bad, making compensation and protecting the child from the consequences of his behavior. The child grows up never learning responsibility and self-control. But when the child is forced to make amends, then she learns an important lesson.

Again John Rosemond illustrates the point. He tells of a neighbor who called him and said his eight-year-old daughter had been disrespectful toward her. Rosemond assured the neighbor that he believed her and that Amy would correct the problem. He then confronted his daughter. When he told Amy he was unhappy about the situation, she began to cry. He told her she had to go and apologize for her disrespect. She begged and pleaded not to have to do that, but her father remained insistent.

When she realized I wasn't going to budge, she composed herself, walked across the street, rang the doorbell, and apologized. As I watched from the living room window, I saw the neighbor smile, take Amy's hand in hers, and nod as if to say that everything was all right.

Amy came back across the street with tears streaming down her face. There were no more punishments, no lectures. In fact, we never again made mention of the situation.

Rosemond says some people object when they hear this story. They say he's laying a guilt trip on his children. And "to a certain extent," he says, "I am."

> When a child does something wrong, she should feel the wrong of what she has done . . . The words you use must come across with enough impact to make the child feel guilty, embarrassed or sorry.[4]

The idea that guilt is bad came out of the "do your own thing" philosophy of the sixties and seventies. The phrase "guilt trip" carries a lot of negative connotations. It is true that extreme guilt is bad; those who are always feeling guilty about things they should not feel guilty about are neurotic. But on the other hand, people who are incapable of feeling any guilt are sociopaths, and they are dangerous to society.

Guilt is a necessary emotion. Without it, civilization as we know it cannot exist. People won't accept responsibility for their own bad behavior unless they feel bad about it. We must train the consciences of our children so that they feel appropriate guilt and understand God's principle: You reap what you sow.

Our job as parents is not only to socialize our children so they can relate to others. More importantly, our job is to spiritualize our children so they can be responsible to God and his Word.

"We must all appear before the judgment seat of Christ, that each one may receive what is due him for the things done while in the body, whether good or bad" (2 Corinthians 5:10).

It is encouraging to see that some young people are proving they are capable of accepting responsibility for their own behavior. The following newspaper article appeared in the Morristown, New Jersey, *Daily Record*:

"No sex, please, we're teenagers." In a rebellion some church leaders hope heralds a new sexual revolution, tens of thousands of young men and women across the country have signed covenants vowing to remain chaste until marriage. By July, organizers of the 'True Love Waits' campaign hope half a million teens will have signed on, filling out enough pledge cards to stretch from the Capitol to the Washington Monument.

The text reads, "Believing that true love waits, I make a commitment to God, myself, my family, those I date and my future children to be sexually pure until the day I enter a covenant marriage relationship."

The campaign began in April as a part of a Southern Baptist Convention sex education program. Adam Allen, 15, of Houston, said the campaign offers a long-awaited opportunity for public redemption to teens portrayed in the media and by some government officials as having out-of-control libidos. "Kids are taught that they're just animals and they're going to have sex—just use a condom," Allen said. "I'm willing to stand by God"[5]

If we are to train our children to be as responsible as Adam Allen and as Moses' sister Miriam, we must saturate them with the Word of God, and we must teach them that they reap what they sow.

---

[1]*John Rosemond's Six-point Plan for Raising Happy, Healthy Children* (Kansas City: Andrews and McMeel, 1989), p. 81. Excerpts used by permission.

[2]*Rosemond's Six-point Plan*, p. 87.

[3]*Rosemond's Six-point Plan*, pp. 90, 91.

[4]*Rosemond's Six-point Plan*, pp. 98, 99.

[5]"A New Sexual Revolution?" *Daily Record*, Parsippany, NJ, September, 1993.

CHAPTER FOUR

Cultivate Respect

Eli and Hophni & Phinehas

1 Samuel 2:12-29

There are four types of authority found in the Bible to which Christians are to be submissive. The first is **divine** authority. Jesus said, "All authority in heaven and on earth has been given to me" (Matthew 28:18). That authority was then delegated to the three other spheres of authority on earth.

There is **civil** authority. Paul commands us in Romans 13:1-7 to submit to the governing authorities. Peter echoes the command in 1 Peter 2:13, 14.

Then there is **church** authority. The Hebrew writer, speaking to the church, said, "Obey your leaders and submit to their authority" (Hebrews 13:17).

The fourth type is **parental** authority. Ephesians 6:1-3 reads,

Children, obey your parents in the Lord, for this is right. Honor your father and mother—which is the first commandment with a promise—"that it may go well with you and that you may enjoy long life on the earth."

We live in an age of disrespect for authority. Today it is common to see people rebelling against all four forms of authority. People mock God, even questioning his existence. Government officials are not trusted, and policemen are viewed as the enemy instead of keepers of the peace. Even the church, once respected in the community as a source of moral authority, is now ridiculed for taking "narrow-minded" stances against immorality.

But the home is where the foundation for learning to respect authority is either strengthened or weakened. Someone said, "As the home goes, so goes the nation." And we see respect for parental authority at an all-time low.

Some time ago, a three-year-old boy in Louisville, Kentucky, took his dad's car out on the street for a joy ride. Mikey Sproul was somehow able to steal his father's keys, get into the car, start it, put it into gear, and send it cruising down the street until it came to a crashing halt. Fortunately no one was harmed. When he was finally stopped, he said to the neighbors, "I go zoom!" Since no one was hurt, it became a humorous incident.

But no one is laughing now. A few weeks later, Mikey set fire to his bedroom curtains with a cigarette lighter and burned down his family's home. His father received third-degree burns while trying to rescue Mikey. State officials have put Mikey in protective care, citing a lack of supervision as the reason for their actions.[1]

The story of Samuel and his faithful mother Hannah is familiar to many. But intertwined in that story is the lesser known story of Eli the priest and his two sons, Hophni and Phinehas. The lessons learned from their negative examples should motivate us to teach our children respect for authority.

Two Disrespectful Sons

Eli held two important positions in Israel: He was both a priest and a judge. In fact, he was a judge for forty years (1 Samuel 4:18). Eli was highly respected. As a man who represented God to the people, he had to be a strong believer and a man of God himself.

Hophni and Phinehas, Eli's sons, followed in his professional footsteps and became priests of the Lord. But the comparison between father and sons stops there.

They Did Not Respect God

"Eli's sons were wicked men; they had no regard for the Lord" (1 Samuel 2:12).

Although they were "P.K.'s" (priest's kids), and priests by profession, in their hearts they were far from God.

They Did Not Respect the House of God

When someone came to the temple to offer sacrifices to God, a portion of the food was to be given to the priests to eat. In the Law of Moses, God had given specific instructions to the priests as to what portion of the sacrifice they were permitted to take (Leviticus 7:28-36). But Eli's sons violated the law and the customs because they wanted the best for themselves.

> But even before the fat was burned, the servant of the priest would come and say to the man who was sacrificing, "Give the priest some meat to roast; he won't accept boiled meat from you, but only raw" (1 Samuel 2:15).

Taking their portion before the fat was burned allowed the corrupt priests to take a bigger and more valuable portion of the meat, thus taking what belonged to God. And if the man giving the sacrifice tried to refuse, Hophni and Phinehas would threaten to take it by force (1 Samuel 2:16). They were making a mockery of the people's worship of God.

> This sin of the young men was very great in the Lord's sight, for they were treating the Lord's offering with contempt (1 Samuel 2:17).

They Did Not Respect Other People

> Now Eli, who was very old, heard about everything his sons were doing to all Israel and how they slept with the women who served at the entrance to the Tent of Meeting (1 Samuel 2:22).

These men, who were supposed to be the spiritual leaders for the entire community, were engaging in illicit sex with the women who came to serve at the tabernacle! Rather than promoting worship and service, they were using their position of authority to take advantage of others and to gratify their own sinful desires. And their sinful actions were common knowledge.

They Did Not Respect Their Father

The underlying cause of their disrespect for God and others was their disrespect for parental authority. Eli rebuked them for all the things he was hearing about them, but they refused to listen (1 Samuel 2:25). Their father's displeasure carried no weight with his sons. They did not even show a hint of respect for him.

Eli was a weak father. Picture the situation: Eli's sons have no respect for God, they have been stealing from the sacrifices, threatening violence against honest worshipers, and sleeping with the temple servant girls. Then Eli says, in essence, "I've been hearing some bad things about you."

At the least, Hophni and Phinehas should have been fired for such misbehavior, even if they were Eli's sons. But Eli's authority was so unimpressive and his sons were so accustomed to ignoring him that their father's rebuke did not even phase them.

The Consequences of Disobedience

God sent a prophet to Eli to pronounce the judgment of God upon Eli's family. He announced that Eli's two sons would die while they were in the prime of life, and that Eli's family would not carry on his legacy as priest because he had neglected to teach his sons respect for authority.

Evidently, during the formative years of his sons' lives, Eli had failed to instill in them proper values. Perhaps his ministry had become more important than his family—or at least seemed to be so from his sons' perspective. Sometimes dads believe their families are more important but act as if their jobs are. A father needs to see himself from his children's perspective and make sure he sends the right message.

When U.S. Representative Ron Mazzoli announced his retirement, many thought the Jefferson County (Kentucky) Commissioner, Irv Maze, would decide to run for Congress to replace him. But Maze changed his mind about the election. He said, "I planned on running, but . . . I couldn't forget something my son said: 'Dad, why don't you stay here and be my baseball coach?'"

Everyone gains respect for a man who has the courage to make that decision. It is a wise parent who can realize the importance of spending time with his children during such impressionable years. Eli apparently failed to understand that truth.

The prophet also told Eli that his two sons would die on the same day. It was a strict judgment, punishing not only the sons, but the father as well.

> This is what the Lord says. . . . "Why do you scorn my sacrifice and offering that I prescribed for my dwelling? Why do you honor your sons more than me. . . ?" (1 Samuel 2:27-29).

Eli was being judged because he honored his sons more than he honored God. What a reminder to parents! While our children are important, our first allegiance must always be to God. That principle is true not only for parents, but for grandparents, uncles, aunts, teachers, and coaches as well. Though we love our children, we must make sure that we honor God first.

In the end, Eli discovered that his passive behavior toward his sons was not the most loving thing he could have done. Both he and his sons had to suffer the consequences. God kept his word. When they were still young men, Hophni and Phinehas died in battle on the same day (1 Samuel 4:11). When the news reached Eli that his sons had died and that the ark of the covenant had been taken, he "fell backward off his chair. . . . His neck was broken and he died, for he was an old man and heavy" (1 Samuel 4:18).

Though parents have the greatest challenge, all adults have a responsibility to teach the children around them to respect authority. All of us who by our actions, examples, and leadership positions have influence over children must be careful to communicate the importance of respect for authority.

Teaching Children to Respect Authority

Dr. Henry Brandt writes this about parenting:

"It starts out as a dream . . . to be the best parent ever! Then the baby arrives . . . and the parents discover that their dream yells, and smells . . . all at three o'clock in the morning."

Suddenly parents realize that rearing a child is much more challenging than they had expected. And one of the most challenging aspects of parenting is teaching your child to respect authority.

Respect Should Be Earned, Not Merely Demanded

Bursts of anger and frustration do not help us gain respect from our children. Parents who lose their temper and shout at their children lose whatever respect their children might once have had for them. DaVinci said, "He who truly knows has no occasion to shout." Our children will respect us if they are confident we truly know and believe in the standards we expect from them.

Trying to intimidate children into obedience is another mistake parents commonly make. Fear teaches a child only to avoid punishment. In such an environment, a child will often learn to avoid punishment by being cunning and crafty instead of learning to be obedient.

Respect must be earned. Children are perceptive and learn by example. They respect adults who model integrity. They will not respect an adult who is constantly communicating, by action or words, "Do as I say, not as I do." Parents cannot expect children to respect their demands that they get along with their siblings if the parents are constantly bickering with one another. A father will have difficulty demanding his son to stay pure if the son can perceive that his father has a lustful eye. We cannot expect children to tell the truth when they hear adults say things like, "Tell them I'm not home."

The same is true when it comes to modeling respect for authority. An adult who is constantly looking for ways to avoid getting caught for speeding, and then degrades the policeman who pulls him over, teaches the children around him something about respect for authority. A mother cannot expect her children to submit to her authority if she refuses to show a submissive attitude toward her husband. When we complain about the decisions the church leaders have made, children are learning something about respect for the authority of the church.

In 1 Corinthians 11:1, Paul says, "Follow my example, as I follow the example of Christ." Actions speak louder than words. Children are much more likely to respect authority if the adults in their lives show them how.

Disrespect Must Be Corrected

There is a temptation for parents to abdicate the teaching of respect for authority to the school, church, or even law enforcers. I have had teachers in our children's and youth departments tell me that they know in a matter of minutes whether a child has been disciplined at home or whether the child rules the roost. But if respect for authority is not taught in the home, it is rarely caught outside the home.

One Christian writer compared the biblical view of discipline to an inverted triangle. In the beginning, the child is given very little freedom, represented by the point of the triangle. As the child grows older, the freedoms become broader and broader, like the base of the triangle. The world's view, on the other hand, is just the opposite. The child is given complete freedom in the beginning because he "doesn't know better." Then, when he becomes a teenager, the parents begin to see the path their child will take if not corrected. They suddenly begin pulling back on the reigns and trying to enforce some boundaries. But by then it is too late.

Two words are key to parental discipline: *consistency* and *communication.*

Without consistency, discipline results in confusion, not respect. Discipline must not just be an occasional act, but a constant factor in all of your parenting or teaching. When a child breaks a rule and receives nothing but threats, the child will continue to test the rule again and again. When discipline finally does come, the child is frustrated because he didn't expect it ever really to happen. Inconsistency will breed exasperation and disrespect in a child, not the respect you desire.

If consistency is to become a part of your discipline techniques, it is important to work on "first-time obedience." If you have to ask a child four or five times to put his toys away, you do not have control of your child. Through his behavior, the child has manipulated you to the point that he is controlling you.

By teaching children to respect parental authority, we are also teaching them a respect for the authority of God. We want children to hear God when he whispers. Parents are sending the wrong message when they allow the child to wait until Mom raises her voice or Dad gets angry before obedience is necessary.

Communication is equally important if we are to discipline our children correctly. Instructions communicated in generalities instead of specifics create an atmosphere of uncertainty.

For example, if a parent commands, "I want you to be good in church," a child does not know what is expected of him. What you call "good" behavior in your three-year-old may not be "good" for your nine-year-old. There need to be specific commands. For instance, a parent may say, "Before we enter the service, you can visit the restroom, then I expect you to sit quietly beside me through the entire service." Punishments for disobedience will vary as well, based upon the severity of the action and the age of the child.

Our associate minister, Dave Stone, shared the following illustration:

> We are currently working on teaching my four-year-old daughter Savannah to respect people by looking them in the eyes when she talks to them. But what happens when she doesn't? Let's say she is in my office when Bob Russell walks by. He stops and says, "You sure look nice today, Savannah."
>
> Savannah is intent on the page she is coloring, and mumbles "Thank you," without even a glance in Bob's direction.
>
> What do I do? Do I spank her and say, "I've told you a hundred times to show respect . . . ?" No; she is in the learning process and trying to remember. I would probably say, "If Mr. Russell was nice enough to take the time to compliment you, it would be right for you to look at him when you tell him, 'Thank you.'"
>
> But let's change the situation. Bob says, "You look nice today, Savannah," and Savannah keeps coloring.
>
> I say, "Savannah, Mr. Russell is talking to you. Can you look at him and tell him, 'Thank you'?"
>
> And she snaps, "No, I don't want to. I'm tired of seeing that old man," then we have a problem. (I'm unemployed!) That would be open defiance or rebellion, and it would be a good time to take her away from people and discipline her so that she knows her behavior is not acceptable and will not be tolerated."[2]

Friendship Should Not Be Achieved Until Adulthood

Parents often make the mistake of trying to be "buddies" with their children too early in life. Friendship should occur when the child reaches adulthood, but if the parent tries to be a friend too early, he loses the chance to teach respect for authority and risks giving the child too much freedom too soon.

In John 15 we read that Jesus brought his twelve closest followers to a new level in their relationship with him. Their discipling process was completed; now he would call them "friends" (John 15:15).

According to Gary and Anne Marie Ezzo, Christian parenting follows the same pattern: Parenting by discipleship. Though there will be plenty of time for friendship later, it is not the starting point. The Ezzos speak of four building block periods that parents pass through with their children. The success of each phase depends on the success of the preceding phase.

The first phase is **discipline.** This occurs from birth through age five. In this phase, your primary goal is to establish your right to rule in the mind of the child. Your task is to get control of the child so you can effectively train him. If you cannot control him, neither you nor anyone else will be able to train him effectively.

The second phase is **training.** This phase takes place from ages six to twelve. The parent is compared to a trainer working with an athlete every day in different settings. The trainer is able to stop the player at any time and make immediate corrections, explaining the reasons for his mistakes, and showing the athlete what to do and how to do it.

The third phase is called the **coaching** phase. It spans from ages thirteen to nineteen. By now, our children are in the game of life themselves. We can send in plays from the sidelines and we can huddle during the time-outs, but we can no longer stop the game and show them how it is to be played. They are now calling the plays themselves and moving forward in life.

The final phase is **friendship.** It is a new season of life, just as it was with the Lord and his disciples. When our children become adults, they should become our friends.[3]

Problems arise when phases are skipped in the parenting process. Consider the following letter to Ann Landers, from a mother who had recently discovered that her eleven-year-old daughter was having sex with her fifteen-year-old boyfriend:

> . . . Although I consider myself open-minded, I have some difficulty with pre-teen sex. . . . I'm confused about what steps to take, if any. I don't want her to think I am "old fashioned."
>
> Carrie is now in sixth grade and very independent. . . . I don't want to ruin our good relationship. What do you think?

Here is Ann Landers' response:

> Dear Mom: Your eleven-year-old daughter is having sex, and you are reluctant to confront her because you don't want to ruin your relationship? Woman, are you out of your mind?
>
> To begin with, an eleven-year-old should not be dating. Permitting her to go with a fifteen-year-old boy strikes me as contributing to the delinquency of a minor.
>
> You need to get some counseling, and so does your daughter. You must learn the basics of responsible parenting, and Carrie needs to be taught that [sexual activity] is not only morally wrong but dangerous.[4]

That mother had obviously skipped some of the phases of parenting. She was trying to be her daughter's friend when she still needed to be the trainer.

Perhaps Eli's sons did not respect him for the same reasons: He attempted to avoid conflict and be their friend. But as a result, he sacrificed their respect.

The Ezzos write, "Parents who try to be buddies early with their child only succeed in raising a fool."

Parents who continue to train and coach their children even when they enter the teen years will surely run into adolescents who want more freedom than they are ready to handle. It is difficult to stick to your convictions when a child is arguing month after month, trying to chip away and gain some compromises. It would be much easier to say, "Well, you're fifteen, it's time to start treating you like an adult."

But that would not be the loving thing for a parent to do. I have often heard young adults express how they wish that their parents would have exerted more authority on them when they were in their teens. They wish that their parents had said "no" more often. They lament that it would have saved them a lot of wasted time, bad memories, and terrible mistakes.

There was some time that elapsed between the prophet's announcement of God's judgment to Eli and the day that it was fulfilled. I wonder what regrets Eli had as he sat and pondered his role as a father. Did he wish he had spent more time with his sons? Did he mourn his failure to set a good example? What regrets must have filled his final days?

It has been said that a parent's role is to give children roots that they might grow and wings that they might fly. It has to be in that order. The roots of discipline must precede the wings of freedom. When a person learns early to respect parents, legal authorities, the church, and God, then a lifetime of productive service is the result. And the parents are left, not with the regrets of Eli, but with many happy memories to fill their final years.

---

[1]*Courier Journal,* Louisville, KY, November 14, 1993.

[2]Used by permission.

[3]Gary and Anne Marie Ezzo, *Preparation for Parenting,* p. 36.

[4]*Courier Journal,* Nov. 16, 1993.

CHAPTER FIVE

Commit to God

Hannah and Samuel

1 Samuel 1-3

A sculptor was being watched by a group of visitors as he chipped and chiseled a block of marble, creating a statue of Abraham Lincoln. After watching him work for some time, a little boy asked, "How did he know President Lincoln was inside that block of marble?"

Who is "inside" your child, waiting to be revealed? A missionary? A president? A loving mother or father? A teacher? A business executive? A preacher?

It is the wish of all Christian parents to lead their children to become godly adults. But achieving that goal is not getting any easier. Dealing with children on a regular basis can be rewarding and thrilling, but it can also be frustrating and stressful.

Most parents and teachers agree that the most frustrating times occur when the child reaches adolescence. The child begins to desire some independence, but he is not yet ready to handle being on his own. As the parents try to find the proper balance between freedom and control, friction can arise and times can be tough.

Mark Twain used to say that when your child reaches the age of twelve you should put him in a barrel and feed him through a knothole; then, when he turns fifteen, seal up the knothole!

But while the adolescent years can be stressful, they can also be some of the most rewarding times of parenting. Perhaps the key is in remembering from the beginning of the child's life that you are not trying to raise a child who will honor you and make you look good, but a child who will honor God. From the beginning, we should be in a process of committing our children to God. Then, when they are older and we release them, we are not turning them loose into the jaws of the world but into the hands of God.

The Old Testament records a dramatic story about a woman named Hannah, who committed her child to God even before he was born. Then she kept her promise by literally giving her son Samuel up to God when he was still a young boy. We can learn from Hannah some valuable lessons about committing our children to God.

The Example of Hannah

In Old Testament times, the greatest calamity a Hebrew woman could face was to be childless. The Hebrews understood that children are a blessing from God.

> Sons are a heritage from the Lord, children a reward from him. Like arrows in the hands of a warrior are sons born in one's youth. Blessed is the man whose quiver is full of them (Psalm 127:3-5).

But the Hebrews wrongly assumed that the antithesis was also true. If children are a blessing from God, then to be childless was considered a curse from God. And Hannah's quiver was empty.

Hannah's Problem

It was bad enough to be childless, but Hannah's pain was compounded by her dysfunctional home life. Her husband Elkanah claimed that he loved her, but she was not his only wife.

Hannah lived in an irreligious time. The people of Israel had lapsed from the high standards of spirituality and morality that Moses had set. Although polygamy was tolerated by the Mosaic law, the Old Testament makes it clear that it was not the original divine arrangement, and it always put an incredible strain on the parties involved.

Adding to the strain, Elkanah's other wife, Peninnah, had several children. And Peninnah was not afraid to call attention to Hannah's weakness. She probably claimed that Hannah was out of God's favor since he had not blessed her with children.

And because the Lord had closed [Hannah's] womb, her rival kept provoking her in order to irritate her. This went on year after year. Whenever Hannah went up to the house of the Lord, her rival provoked her till she wept and would not eat (1 Samuel 1:6, 7).

Hannah's Promise

When Hannah was in the house of the Lord, she prayed that God would grant her a child. She promised that if she were given a son, she would dedicate that child completely to the service of God.

And she made a vow, saying, "O Lord Almighty, if you will only look upon your servant's misery and remember me, and not forget your servant but give her a son, then I will give him to the Lord for all the days of his life . . ." (1 Samuel 1:11).

Hannah was not praying aloud, but she was moving her lips while she wept and prayed from her heart. When Eli the priest saw Hannah praying, he thought she was drunk! Many Israelites had turned away from God in those days, and there apparently was not much heartfelt praying going on in the house of the Lord.

Eli confronted Hannah, so she explained that she was not drunk. Instead, she said, "I have been praying here out of my great anguish and grief" (1 Samuel 1:15, 16).

When Eli realized her sincerity, he said to her, "Go in peace, and may the God of Israel grant you what you have asked of him" (1 Samuel 1:17).

The Bible says that the Lord remembered Hannah, and she conceived and gave birth to a son. They named him Samuel, which means "heard of God," because she had asked the Lord for him (1 Samuel 1:20).

Hannah's Commitment

Hannah dearly loved Samuel, but from his birth she prepared him to be used of God.

When the man Elkanah went up with all his family to offer the annual sacrifice to the Lord and to fulfill his vow, Hannah did not go. She said to her husband, "After the boy is weaned, I will take him and present him before the Lord, and he will live there always."

"Do what seems best to you," Elkanah her husband told her. "Stay here until you have weaned him; only may the Lord make good his word." So the woman stayed at home and nursed her son until she had weaned him (1 Samuel 1:21-23).

God had given Hannah the desire of her heart. She knew she could show her appreciation to God by keeping her promise, as painful as that would be.

After he was weaned, she took the boy with her, young as he was. . . . They brought the boy to Eli, and she said to him, "As surely as you live, my lord, I am the woman who stood here beside you praying to the Lord. I prayed for this child, and the Lord has granted me what I asked of him. So now I give him to the Lord. For his whole life he will be given over to the Lord" (1 Samuel 1:24-28).

We don't know exactly how old Samuel was. It appears he was old enough to care for himself and old enough to be a helper in the tabernacle. He may have been seven or eight years old, or perhaps a little older, but he was still very young for his mother to completely release the son she loved so much.

Hannah was able to see Samuel only once a year.

Each year his mother made him a little robe and took it to him when she went up with her husband to offer the annual sacrifice (1 Samuel 2:19).

Can't you picture Hannah spending hours on a new robe for her son Samuel, thinking about him, wondering how he was doing, trying to speculate how much he had grown since last year?

We rarely see that kind of commitment to God today. People might be radically committed to other things, like their job or a hero or their favorite sports team, but rarely do we see people willing to make that kind of sacrifice for God.

In Kentucky, there is a huge rivalry in college basketball between the University of Louisville and the University of Kentucky. The story is told that at one of the recent "Dream Games" between the two schools, an elderly woman was sitting alone with an empty seat next to her. Someone approached her and said, "Ma'am, I have rarely seen an empty seat in Rupp Arena, let alone at the Dream Game. Whose seat is this?

The woman responded that she and her late husband had been season ticket holders for twenty-eight years, and the seat had belonged to him. "Well, couldn't you find a friend or relative to come to the game with you?" the observer asked.

"Are you kidding?" She replied. "They're all at my husband's funeral!"

Hannah knew where her commitments needed to be. Her ability to release her child to God should be a reminder to all Christian parents.

Committing Our Children to God

Our church does not sprinkle or baptize babies. It has been our commitment to baptize only adult believers as was the pattern in the New Testament. However, we began to realize that parents had no way of expressing to the church their desires to commit themselves and their children to the Lord. So we began having a periodic baby-dedication service. It is a beautiful and simple ceremony where the parents and infants come before the congregation, the church prays for the parents, and the parents commit to raising their children to know the Lord. It is a reminder that even from the beginning of a child's life, the parents' goal is to commit that child to the Lord.

Wayne Smith, the minister of the Southland Christian Church in Lexington, Kentucky, was brought up in a Christian home. When his parents died, they hardly had anything to leave for their children because they had always been poor. Wayne said, "My parents didn't leave me a farm, they left me a faith."

If we could see things from God's perspective, every parent would want the same for his children. Leaving a wealthy inheritance is nothing compared to leaving a heritage of faith. However, that heritage is never left by accident. It only happens when parents have committed themselves and their children to God.

Commit Your Child to God by Prayer

Greg Johnson and Mike Yorkey, in their book *Faithful Parents, Faithful Kids,* compiled hundreds of interviews with Christian adults who were reared in Christian homes. When they were asked how their parents had pointed them to Christ, here were some of their answers:

> "When my dad would pray with me at bedtime, he'd always ask God to help make him a better dad. That showed me he wasn't perfect and really wanted God's hand in his life."
> "We always had family devotions."
> "I'd often see Mom and Dad up early on their knees. This evoked a great amount of love from me for them. I knew they were praying for their children."[1]

I can recall similar experiences in my own life. Hannah committed Samuel to God in prayer long before she released him to be God's servant. Prayer, with your children and for your children, is the first step in committing them to God. Your children need to hear you pray and they need to know you are praying for them. And God will answer your prayer.

Lead Your Child to God by Intent

It is never an accident when a child is reared to honor God. Sam Stone said, "Homes don't just happen." If you raise your child to know God, there is no guarantee that he will always follow God faithfully, because every individual is responsible for his or her own actions. But more often than not, children will follow their parents' desires.

What is the most important thing a parent should want for her children? Some want their children to have a better life than they had. They want their children to have plenty of material wealth so they can live life comfortably. But Jesus said,

> Watch out! Be on your guard against all kinds of greed; a man's life does not consist in the abundance of his possessions (Luke 12:15).

Others want to raise their children to be accepted into a top college when they graduate, that they might have the best education money can buy. But Solomon said,

The fear of the Lord is the beginning of knowledge (Proverbs 1:7).

Some parents want their children to be well-liked, to have plenty of friends and no enemies. But Jesus said,

Woe to you when all men speak well of you (Luke 6:26).

Many parents desire children who will grow to be attractive or athletic, and who will marry an attractive spouse. But God said,

Do not consider his appearance or his height. . . . The Lord does not look at the things man looks at. Man looks at the outward appearance, but the Lord looks at the heart (1 Samuel 16:7).

What should Christian parents desire most for their children? They should desire that their children know Jesus Christ, that they might better handle the failures and successes of this world, and more importantly, that they might spend eternity in heaven.

Anne Ortlund wrote,

Parents, you and I are from a different world. And our responsibility is to prepare out children for a world where we cannot go—not so they will be rich or famous or happy, but so they will know the Lord.[2]

Every parent must constantly evaluate what he really wants for his children. What desires are you communicating to your kids? "What good will it be for a man if he gains the whole world, yet forfeits his soul?" (Matthew 16:26).

Release Your Child to God by Faith

The most difficult day in Hannah's life had to have been the day she took Samuel to the house of God, introduced him to Eli, and then walked away. If you have ever experienced taking a child to the first day of kindergarten or the first day of college, or loading up your child's belongings on a U-Haul and watching him or her drive off to a new home, you can relate to Hannah.

But as one psychologist said, "It is the basic job of the parents to get the children out of our lives." Many parents make the mistake of trying to hold on to their children too long, even making them feel guilty for moving away from home, getting married, or not visiting their parents frequently enough.

For the first few years of our marriage, my wife and I made the effort to visit our parents' homes at Christmastime. Judy's parents lived in central Indiana, a few hours from our home in Louisville, and mine lived in northern Pennsylvania, almost ten hours away. Those trips were long and became even longer once we had children of our own. One Christmas Judy and I began to discuss the possibility of staying home the next year. I approached my mother, thinking I had better delicately plant the seed, and I said, "Mom, Judy and I have been talking about what we're going to do at Christmastime next year."

She interrupted and said, "I'll tell you what you should do: You should stay home and start your own traditions. The reason you always liked Christmas here is because we stayed home. You need to do the same for your kids."

I was so relieved! The next year we began staying home, and we developed some wonderful Christmas traditions. We may not visit my parents' home as often as we used to, but when we do, they know we are there because we want to be. They now come to visit us as often as they can, and we have continued to have an excellent relationship.

The first priority of the parents is to raise their children to know the Lord. The second priority is to release them at the proper time back to the Lord.

That takes a lot of faith on the part of the parents. It is risky. But as Zig Ziglar said, it is risky when a ship leaves the harbor, but that is what a ship is for. A ship that never leaves the harbor is not good for anything.

It is risky when a plane leaves the runway, but that is what a plane is for. A plane that never leaves the runway is not good for anything.

It is risky when you release your child to the Lord. It takes faith that God will take care of your child. But that is why the child was born. Commit the child to God in prayer, lead the child to God by showing him your godly intentions for his life, and then—at the proper time—release your child to God by faith.

Who knows? There may just be a "Samuel" inside your child waiting to be released!

---

[1]Greg Johnson and Mike Yorkey, *Faithful Parents, Faithful Kids* (Wheaton: Tyndale House, 1993), pp. 345, 346.

[2]Anne Ortlund, *Disciplines of the Home* (Dallas: Word, 1991).

CHAPTER SIX

Develop Courage

David

1 Samuel 16:1, 6-23

In Jackson, Mississippi, nearly 200 Winfield High School students walked out of classes one day in support of their principal, Bishop Knox. According to an Associated Press Article, Knox was fired for allowing a student to read a brief prayer over the public address system. School officials suspended the students for three days as discipline for their protest.

Joanie Dalton, a ninth grader, said, "We are trying to prove that school prayer is right. We need it. Maybe there wouldn't be as much crime."[1]

Another report on the same day told about a Grand Rapids, Michigan, judge who ordered a picture of Jesus removed from a high school hallway. He rejected a compromise that would have placed the pictures of other historical figures along with the picture of Jesus, saying it was a violation of the separation of church and state.[2]

Most of us have not had to face much persecution in our lives. We have lived in an abnormal time when our culture has been generally supportive of Christians. Most of us have not had our lives threatened, and our beliefs are seldom challenged.

However, we are entering a post-Christian era, and the mood of our culture is rapidly changing. A recent Gallup survey suggested that only one in ten Americans is a committed

Christian. If anti-Christian feelings continue to intensify, our children will face increased opposition and persecution. But that is just what Paul warned us to expect: "Everyone who wants to live a godly life in Christ Jesus will be persecuted" (2 Timothy 3:12).

In the future, a school teacher who talks about Christ might lose her job. A businessman who refuses to employ a homosexual may be boycotted or fined. A professor who believes in creation may be dropped from the faculty. A preacher or writer who shares the absolute truth of Scripture may be taken to court for using "inflammatory" or "politically incorrect" language.

Although we have not experienced much persecution in America, facing persecution has been the norm for most Christians throughout history. Jesus said, "If the world hates you, keep in mind that it hated me first" (John 15:18).

The next generation of Christians will likely face much more persecution than we have faced, and they will need a mental, physical, and spiritual toughness we have not had. If we are going to be successful in passing the baton of faith, we need to impart to our children a sense of courage.

The Old Testament character David developed courage in his youth. He lived in a precarious time that repeatedly tested his mettle. He was a spirited young man who stood firm for his faith in spite of fearful opposition, and he became the greatest leader the nation of Israel had ever known.

By studying the example of David, perhaps we can learn how to develop courage in the lives of our children.

David's Advantages

> The Lord said to Samuel, "How long will you mourn for Saul, since I have rejected him as king over Israel? Fill your horn with oil and be on your way; I am sending you to Jesse of Bethlehem. I have chosen one of his sons to be king" (1 Samuel 16:1).

David Grew Up in the Country

There are several advantages to growing up in the country. It has already been mentioned that young people who grow up in rural areas normally have chores to do, and this teaches them to take responsibility. David grew up in the country and had to tend sheep and run errands for his father.

Growing up in the country also encourages rugged individualism. Parents who raise their children in rural areas can allow their children to explore on their own in an environment of limited risks. I can remember building a dam in the creek, swimming in a farm pond, jumping fifteen feet down into a hay mow, riding a horse that was not fully broken, getting on the back of a young calf, hunting rabbits, walking through the woods at night, and driving the tractor.

Parents in the city tend to be overprotective. There are drunk drivers, rapists, child molesters, and street gangs with which to contend. David told of killing a lion and a bear that attacked his sheep (1 Samuel 17:34-36), so there are certainly dangers in the country, too. But for the most part, the dangers in the country are less menacing and not as constant as dangers can be in the city.

Suburban parents should look for opportunities that allow their children to take some reasonable risks so that they can develop a courageous spirit. Swimming or diving lessons, learning to drive a car, playing football, performing in a talent show, shopping on their own, or riding the bus by themselves helps them develop self-confidence and courage. One family in our church decided to allow their teenage daughter to go bungee jumping. The parents were terrified, but they knew that children need to learn they can face danger and conquer it.

Local sponsors recently removed their support from Kentucky's state spelling bee. They claimed that a spelling bee places incredible stress on students. Somebody needs to tell those people that life has stress! Not everyone who campaigns for an election gets elected. Not everyone who applies gets the job. The doctor does not always have good news. If we eliminate all stress and competition, we limit our students to a level of mediocrity and fail to prepare them for the stresses they will face in life.

David Grew Up in a Large Family

David was the youngest of eight brothers. He was probably teased and shoved around and left out by his brothers when they were growing up. If you had lived next door to David, you might have felt sorry for him. But being the youngest of eight brothers forced David to be more courageous.

When Judy and I were first married, I wanted to have five or six children. I had always felt that my growing up in a family of six children was a great advantage, and I wanted my children to have the same advantage.

But our first child was a breech birth, and my wife was in labor for twenty-four hours. When our second child, Phil, was born, he weighed over ten pounds. Judy looked at me from the hospital bed and said two words that changed my thinking: "Never again."

Though we decided not to have more children, we knew that children who grow up in a large family naturally learn some lessons that we would have to take special care to teach our children. Children in larger families are forced to share, so they learn quickly that they are not the center of the universe. They also learn the art of self-protection. If you don't stand up for yourself in a large family, you will get run over! Children learn the hard way to be courageous.

One of the dangers we must guard against in smaller families is giving our children too much attention. Consider the following *USA Today* article entitled, "Parenting Spiraling Out of Control,"

> Parents want the brightest, most talented children they can possibly produce. Some are into flash cards for six month old infants, and they psychoanalyze every playground encounter. They compare report cards and censor friends in the first grade. They consume books on parenting for advanced children and take them to a different school activity five nights a week when they're in the fifth grade, to make sure they're active and popular.
>
> Everyone is into overparenting. Our theme song is Sting's theme to obsession. "Every breath you take, every move you make, I'll be watching you."
>
> . . . . Overparenting is based on insecurity and low self esteem of the parents, and an inability to recognize the kid is a separate human being.[3]

In small families, parents commonly make the mistake of creating a home that is child-centered, focusing everything on the child and forcing even the marriage to take second place. Children need the security of knowing the home is centered on the marriage. Too much attention on a child can be as damaging as too much food. A child can begin to think the world revolves around him, which can cause many psychological, emotional, and spiritual problems later in life.

> Our children's ultimate task is to move away from us, and our task is to help them. . . . A child cannot be the center of attention in a family and move away from that center at the same time. It's either one or the other.[4]

Wise parents will take specific measures to be sure they have a marriage-centered home. They will not ignore or neglect their children, but they will not allow the children to become the center of attention. Such measures might include the following:
- Don't allow the child to interrupt every conversation.
- Create a weekly night out for the parents, leaving the child(ren) with a baby-sitter
- Put children to bed early enough that the parents have time to enjoy each other.
- At church, put young children in the nursery or children's class, even though they may initially cry or be fearful.

Respected psychiatrist Dr. Frank Minirth and pediatrician Dr. Paul Warren have written a helpful book for teaching young children to overcome their fears. The book is titled, *Things That Go Bump In the Night.* In it they explain that a child's first fear is the fear of abandonment, which is closely tied to the child's sense of identity. A doctor will hold a newborn baby and then abruptly lower his hands a few inches to see whether the baby's arms flail and its mouth flies open. A baby's healthy fear of falling and of being left alone is a sign to the doctor that the baby is normal.[5]

If a parent never leaves a child, it actually increases the child's fear of being abandoned. Minirth and Warren suggest that parents should begin leaving a child temporarily on occasion so that the child can learn to grow through his fear. The child needs to be taught that the parents will eventually return, and that separation is normal.

No one is suggesting that parents selfishly neglect their children, like those who have left their young children home alone for days while they went on vacation. But parents must learn not to overparent. For the child's sake as well as their own, parents must give more attention to the marriage than they do to the child.

The divorce rate among people forty-five and older has been accelerating faster than for any other age group. This group has focused so much on being good parents that they've forgotten how to be partners. When the children are grown and leave home, the parents are apparently unable to maintain their own relationship. Husbands and wives must ensure that, when the children leave, they still have a relationship on which to build. Single parents also need to develop interests apart from their children. This is good for the children and for their own well-being.

My parents loved me a lot, but they also gave me the security of knowing that their marriage was more important to them than I was. I would see them on a beautiful spring Sunday afternoon walk off toward the woods, holding hands. I would ask, "Can I come, too?"

"No," they would answer. "This is just for the two of us." I couldn't understand then why they wouldn't let me go. But now I'm fifty years old, I've been married for twenty-eight years, and we've raised two children of our own. Now I understand they needed to get away from us for a while!

My parents had another way of instilling in me courage and self-reliance. As I was growing up, they would say to me, "When you are eighteen years old and you graduate from high school, you are expected to go to college or to get a job and be gone from home." That wasn't harsh or unkind. It was a reminder that at a specific point in my life, I was expected to grow up and learn to live on my own. To allow me to do otherwise would have been less than loving.

David's Anointing

God informed Samuel that King Saul's successor would come from the household of Jesse. So Samuel went to Jesse's home and asked to see his sons.

Anointed Because of His Heart

> When they arrived, Samuel saw Eliab [Jesse's oldest son] and thought, "Surely the Lord's anointed stands here before the Lord" (1 Samuel 16:6).

The Bible implies that Samuel was impressed with Eliab because he had a good appearance and he was tall.

There are five men on our church staff that are six-feet, four-inches tall or taller. Their mothers neglected to take them to height watchers when they were growing up. I am five-nine, which is considered average height in America, but I take a lot of teasing from those guys. I always thought a man was measured from the neck up, but they don't seem to think so.

Dr. Marshall Leggett, the president of Milligan College, is five-six. He claims that the person most discriminated against in America is not the black person or the native American or the woman, but the short person. People insult short people without even realizing it. There are common syntax slurs: If you admire someone, you look up to him. If you have no regard for someone, you look down on him. If someone is generous, he's a big giver. If he is selfish, he is little. If you want to make fun of someone, you belittle him. Dr. Leggett says, "Just once, I'd like to be-big somebody!"

Athletics discriminate against short people. They say, "He's too short to play center on the basketball team," or "The quarterback's too little to see over the linemen." Literature discriminates, too. Many of us had to memorize the poem: "God, give us men. Times like these demand tall men who see above the clouds." The obvious implication is that short people live in the fog!

Even the Bible discriminates against short people, and that really hurts! The Bible says, "The wicked will be cut short"!

Dr. Leggett has said he is going to organize a "Society of Zaccheus." The sycamore tree will be our emblem, and our motto will be, "Little is lovely, puny is pretty, and small beats all." We will have our own poem: "God, give us men. Times like these demand short men, down-to-earth men who see things as they really are."

Samuel had made a common mistake. People tend to assume that tall people will automatically make good leaders.

But the Lord said to Samuel, "Do not consider his appearance or his height, for I have rejected him. The Lord does not look at the things man looks at. Man looks at the outward appearance, but the Lord looks at the heart" (1 Samuel 16:7).

Seven of Jesse's sons were paraded past Samuel, but none of them met God's requirements. That's when Samuel asked Jesse if someone were missing.

"There is still the youngest," Jesse answered, "but he is tending the sheep" (1 Samuel 16:11).

No one could imagine that young David could end up being anybody special. But as Ray Boltz sang, "When others see a shepherd boy, God may see a king"[6]

Samuel said, "Send for him; we will not sit down until he arrives."
So he sent and had him brought in. He was ruddy, with a fine appearance and handsome features.
Then the Lord said, "Rise and anoint him; he is the one" (1 Samuel 16:11, 12).

David may have been but a youth, but he had a fine appearance and much charisma. More important, he was "a man after [God's] own heart" (1 Samuel 13:14).

Anointed for a Spiritual Purpose

So Samuel took the horn of oil and anointed him in the presence of his brothers, and from that day on the Spirit of the Lord came upon David in power (1 Samuel 16:13).

You can imagine what Samuel's anointing did to David's level of confidence. The second most influential man in Israel, the man considered to be God's messenger, was insisting that David had been called by God for a special purpose: to be the next king of Israel.

One of the ways that we can develop courage in young people is by anointing them with a spiritual purpose. Everyone knows the importance of positive affirmation. We say to children, "What a nice coloring job!" "You're a good reader." "You really hustled today!" "You must practice the piano for hours to be able to play like that." We know that encouragement is a tremendous incentive for future effort and achievement.

But as Christians, we should also be alert for opportunities to boost a child's courage. 1 Thessalonians 5:14 says, "Encourage the timid." The word *encourage* literally means "to instill courage."

Parents need to say to their children, "I noticed that you told the truth when it would have been easy to lie. That took a lot of courage." Christian coaches and teachers need to say, "I noticed you didn't retaliate when you were ridiculed. That took guts." Grandparents and relatives should also leap at the opportunity to encourage. "I heard you give the prayer at the dinner table. You did a good job. It takes courage to pray in front of all your relatives."

When I was in the first grade, I quoted ten verses of Scripture at the opening exercises of our Sunday school program. Our minister, D. P. Shaffer, who was eighty years old, stopped me in the hallway afterwards. He bent down, putting his trembling hand on my shoulder, and said, "Is this the boy who quoted from John 14 this morning? Young man, you could make a good preacher some day!" Over a decade later, in my senior year of high school, the seed that Brother Shaffer had planted in my mind finally took root. I decided to enter the ministry. You do not know how God may be using you to anoint a young person with a courageous purpose through your encouraging words.

David's Accomplishments

King Saul became troubled by an evil spirit. Saul's attendants suggested that someone be brought in to play soothing music for the king, thinking that would calm his spirit. One of the servants suggested David for the task. "[He] knows how to play the harp. He is a brave man and a warrior. He speaks well and is a fine-looking man. And the Lord is with him" (1 Samuel 16:18). David performed his task so well that Saul came to like him and made him one of his armor-bearers (1 Samuel 16:21).

It took courage for a shepherd boy to play for an emotionally unstable king. We see young people get nervous when they play an instrument in a recital when only their relatives and a few close friends are present. David was playing before the king of Israel. And Saul was such a volatile person that if he didn't like the music, David could be humiliated or even executed. But David courageously performed his task well.

Then came that famous day when David faced Goliath. David's older brothers were fighting the Philistines, and David's father sent him to find out about the battle. When David arrived, he was intrigued by the drama before him. A Philistine man, Goliath, who was nearly ten feet tall, would come down daily to the valley between the two camps and dare any Israelite to fight him.

> "If he is able to fight me and kill me, we will become your subjects; but if I overcome him and kill him, you will become our subjects and serve us." . . .
> On hearing the Philistine's words, Saul and all the Israelites were dismayed and terrified (1 Samuel 17:9, 11).

David began quizzing the soldiers for information: "What has the king promised to give anyone who will fight the giant? Wow! No kidding? Great Wealth! Exemption from taxes for his family! The king's daughter in marriage! Why doesn't someone take that giant on? God will certainly give the victory."

But David's brothers became angry with him for being so brazen.

> When Eliab, David's oldest brother, heard him speaking with the men, he burned with anger at him and asked, "Why have you come down here? And with whom did you leave those few sheep in the desert? I know how conceited you are and how wicked your heart is; you came down only to watch the battle" (1 Samuel 17:28).

David was not intimidated by the ridicule of his older brother.

> "Now what have I done?" said David. "Can't I even speak?" He then turned away to someone else and brought up the same matter, and the men answered him as before (1 Samuel 17:29, 30).

Saul heard that the young man was asking questions, so he sent for David, who immediately volunteered to fight the giant.

> Saul replied, "You are not able to go out against this Philistine and fight him; you are only a boy, and he has been a fighting man from his youth" (1 Samuel 17:33).

David told Saul how as a shepherd boy he had killed a lion and a bear with his own hands. Then he said,

"This uncircumcised Philistine will be like one of them, because he has defied the armies of the living God. The Lord who delivered me from the paw of the lion and the paw of the bear will deliver me from the hand of this Philistine."

Saul said to David, "Go, and the Lord be with you" (1 Samuel 17:36, 37).

Others were terrified of Goliath, thinking he was so big they could never defeat him. David thought, "He's so big, how could I miss?"

With thousands of soldiers from both sides watching, David chose five smooth stones from the creek bed. When Goliath saw that they had sent only a boy to meet him, he was insulted.

He said to David, "Am I a dog, that you come at me with sticks?" And the Philistine cursed David by his gods. "Come here," he said, "and I'll give your flesh to the birds of the air and the beasts of the field!"

David said to the Philistine, "You come against me with sword and spear and javelin, but I come against you in the name of the Lord Almighty, the God of the armies of Israel, whom you have defied. This day the Lord will hand you over to me, and I'll strike you down and cut off your head. Today I will give the carcasses of the Philistine army to the birds of the air and the beasts of the earth, and the whole world will know that there is a God in Israel. All those gathered here will know that it is not by sword or spear that the Lord saves; for the battle is the Lord's, and he will give all of you into our hands'" (1 Samuel 17:43-47).

We all know the rest of the story. As Goliath lumbered toward him, David ran after the giant. He reached into his bag and took out a stone, loading it into his sling. Then he hurled it at Goliath, striking him in the forehead. And Goliath fell facedown to the ground.

So David triumphed over the Philistine with a sling and a stone; without a sword in his hand he struck down the Philistine and killed him (1 Samuel 17:50).

Our Duty: Expose Children to Examples of Courage

Young people today need to be exposed to courageous heroes like David, who took a stand for God's truth. Children are being brainwashed by our society into believing that there is no truth worth standing up for, and certainly none worth dying for. If our children's only heroes are Michael Jackson and Madonna, they will have no spiritual incentive. We must instill in them a love for the great spiritual heroes of the past.

We should tell them about Moses, who chose to suffer affliction with the people of God rather than enjoy the pleasures of sin for a season.

We should read to them about Joseph, who resisted Potiphar's wife even though he went to jail for it.

We should let them know about Daniel, who prayed even when it was against the law, and he was thrown into a den of lions.

And we should tell them about David, who fought against the giant Goliath because he knew God was on his side.

I can remember as a young boy, listening to my mother teach me about Jesus calming the storm. She told me that the disciples were afraid of a terrible storm that had come upon the Sea of Galilee. They awakened Jesus and said, "Don't you care if we die?" Jesus rebuked the disciples, and then calmed the sea.

I said to my mother, "Weren't the disciples silly to be afraid when they had Jesus with them in the boat? God wasn't going to let Jesus drown."

"Right, Bobby," she said. "And you remember that God is always with you, too. You don't ever need to be afraid."

We should tell our children of other great spiritual heroes, even those not mentioned in the Bible.

The book of 2 Maccabees, chapter seven, relates the terrible persecution that the Jews suffered under Antiochus IV Epiphanes nearly 200 years before Christ. Antiochus decided that if the Jews would not adopt the Greek way of life, he would force them to give up their religion. Whatever the Torah commanded the Jews not to do, Antiochus would command them to do. Those who refused were executed.

Antiochus's officials were ordered to sacrifice a pig on the altar of the temple, which to the Jews was the worst possible sacrilege. Antiochus then forced many Jews to eat one of the sacrificed pigs. That, too, was a horrible sacrilege.

A mother had seven sons who were all ordered to eat the swine. When the oldest son refused, his head was scalped, his tongue was cut out, his hands and feet were cut off, and then he was burned to death.

The soldiers then came to the second son, who also refused, and the process was repeated. The same was true for the third, fourth, fifth and sixth sons. All of them stubbornly refused to deny their God, and suffered the same consequences.

The seventh son was a young boy. The officer pleaded with the mother, "Please, just tell your son to touch the pork to his lips, and we will let him go."

The mother agreed to talk to her son, but she did not tell him to do what they had asked. Brokenhearted, she spoke to him in the language of her people, "My son, have pity on me. I carried you for nine months in my womb and nursed you for three years. I have reared you for this moment. I urge you to look to the heavens and the earth and remember that they were not made by human hands. Do not fear these butchers, but prove worthy of your brothers. Accept death, so that in God's mercy I may get you back again with your brothers."

The boy turned to the officer, put out his hands and said, "The God who gave these to me once will give them back again." He was brutally executed.

The historian wrote, "So he died in his integrity, putting his trust in the Lord." Lastly, the mother was killed also. The historian said, "Filled with a noble spirit, she fired her woman's reasoning with a man's courage."

It was that story that Judas Maccabees used as a rallying cry for the Maccabean revolt in 165 B.C. The Jews stormed into Jerusalem and threw out the Greeks who had defiled their temple. Jerusalem was free again for the first time in 400 years.

Do your children know about Martin Luther, who studied the Bible and defied the errors of the church of the dark ages? Have they heard how he stood before the court at Worms, threatened with death if he did not renounce the things he had written, and said, "Unless I am persuaded by Scripture, . . . I cannot and will not revoke anything. God help me. Amen"?

Do they know the courage of men like Patrick Henry, who said, "Give me liberty or give me death"?

Do they know about Corrie Ten Boom and the Hiding Place, where she and her family hid dozens of Jews fleeing the terror of the Nazis, though it eventually cost them their freedom and cost many of them their lives?

We should brag about contemporary Christian heroes and stop belittling Christian leaders. Some of them need to be held up for our children to admire and emulate.

Invite Christians into your home and say to your children, "That man is one of the smartest people I know, and he is a believer in Christ."

"That guy is really rich, but he is so generous with his money."

"She could be making millions singing in the secular world, but she is singing for the Lord."

"He is so funny he could be a stand-up comedian, but he has chosen to be a preacher. He uses his humor to keep people's attention so he can tell them about Christ."

More importantly, they need to hear how your family has endured stress and hard times. I tried to remember to tell my boys: "Did you know that Grandma and Grandpa endured the Great Depression? They had almost no money, and they ate beans and cornbread every day. But they kept on tithing what they had and giving it to the church. Then they invited my uncle Ralph to live with them because he had no job. Your grandpa worked twelve hours a day and walked home in the dark three miles to keep the family going."

Most importantly, your children need to see how you respond to pressure. When there is a frightening experience, do you curse God and swear, or do they see you praying, trusting God and maintaining your composure?

Sam Stone is the editor of a Christian journal, *Christian Standard*. Several years ago, he and his family were involved in a serious automobile accident. It was a head-on collision and his wife was nearly killed. His son Dave, now an associate minister at the church I serve, was just six years old at the time. He says the accident left an indelible impression on his memory—especially in how his parents immediately responded to the crisis.

After the accident, my brother and I were not hurt. But I looked up, and my Dad's glasses were broken and cockeyed. My mother was bleeding profusely. I remember hearing in the distance the sirens of the emergency vehicles. Then I remember hearing my Dad quote the Twenty-third Psalm. "The Lord is my Shepherd, I shall not want. He makes me to lie down in green pastures, he leads me beside the still waters, he restores my soul. He leads me in the paths of righteousness for his name's sake. Yea, though I walk through the valley of the shadow of death, I will fear no evil, for Thou art with me. Thy rod and thy staff, they comfort me. . . ."

When the sirens are blowing in your life, what do your children hear you say?

Jesus said, "Do not be afraid of what you are about to suffer. I tell you, the devil will put some of you in prison to test you, and you will suffer persecution for ten days. Be faithful, even to the point of death, and I will give you the crown of life" (Revelation 2:10).

No one ever demonstrated more courage than Jesus Christ. He stood before Pilate and was asked, "Are you a king?" If he had hedged just a little, Pilate would have set him free.

But Jesus said boldly, "I am." And for the truth, and for our sins, he died.

May all who come behind us find us faithful.

----

[1]*Houston Post,* November 30, 1993.

[2]Ibid.

[3]*USA Today,* July 28, 1993. Copyright 1993, USA TODAY. Reprinted with permission.

[4]*Rosemond's Six-point Plan,* p. 10.

[5]Minirth and Warren, *Things That Go Bump In the Night,* pages 23, 24.

[6]"Shepherd Boy," 1988, Gaither Music.

CHAPTER SEVEN

Build a
Friendship

David and Jonathan

1 Samuel 18:1-4; 20:1-42

Even Jesus needed friends. He had twelve close friends, the twelve apostles, whom he chose "that they might be with him" (Mark 3:14). He wanted them with him to train them to serve, but there was also a matter of fellowship. Three of the apostles formed an "inner circle"; they were Jesus' closest friends. He spent more time with Peter, James, and John and included them in more activities. (See Mark 5:37; 9:2; 14:33.) Among those three, John called himself "the disciple whom Jesus loved" (John 13:23). Apparently, Jesus even had a "best friend."

Jesus had other friends with whom he felt a special bond. Mary, Martha, and Lazarus lived in Bethany, just outside of Jerusalem. They showed him excellent hospitality and he visited them often (John 11:5). Lazarus was known to Jesus as "the one you love" (John 11:3). Jesus also enjoyed visiting in the homes of Zacchaeus, Simon the leper, and others.

If Jesus needed friends, how much more do the rest of us! Someone said the most desperate word in the English language is the word *loneliness.* We all need people who care about us, people with whom we can relax and be ourselves.

Although you will lose your effectiveness as a parent if you try to be "friends" with your children while they are young, you will also lose your child's respect if you never allow your relationship to reach the friendship level once the child becomes an adult. That is the reason we need to consider the relationship between a parent and the adult child. What happens when the training stage is over? The best way to be a positive influence in your child's life after he or she has left home is to quit trying to be a parent, a trainer, or even a coach, and to see your child as another adult who needs a friend.

Emerson said, "If you want to have a friend, be one." If you want your children to come around after they have moved away, learn to be a friend.

There are different levels of friendship. We have *casual friends*, people whose company we enjoy only occasionally. Co-workers are often casual friends. We see them on the job and we get along well, but we normally don't see them any other time and therefore do not develop a closer friendship. We also have *close friends*, people whom we see more frequently and with whom we have a deeper bond of fellowship. We make time for close friends. We need the fellowship we share when we are together. Then there are *intimate friends*, those with whom we feel a deep interweaving of soul. These are the friends with whom we can be completely open and honest, from whom we hide nothing.

Over the course of a lifetime a person may have only a couple of intimate friends. And on those rare occasions when it occurs within the family—a husband and wife have an intimate friendship, or a parent and adult child share such a deep relationship—it is especially rewarding.

The greatest example of intimate friendship in the Old Testament is the story of Jonathan and David, two young men who, because of their circumstances, might well have hated each other. By the grace of God, however, they became the closest of friends.

From every angle it would seem that Jonathan and David would be natural rivals. Jonathan was the oldest son of King Saul: the crown prince, the heir to the throne of Israel. However, David, a shepherd boy, had been anointed by the prophet Samuel to become the next king instead of Jonathan. You would think they would despise one another. Jonathan, especially, would see David as an obvious threat to his future. Instead, Jonathan became David's most loyal friend.

Friends Are Loyal

After David had finished talking with Saul, Jonathan became one in spirit with David, and he loved him as himself. . . . And Jonathan made a covenant with David because he loved him as himself. Jonathan took off the robe he was wearing and gave it to David, along with his tunic, and even his sword, his bow and his belt (1 Samuel 18:1-4).

This was no ordinary gift exchange!

It is considered in the East a special mark of respect to be presented by a prince with some of the garments he has for his own wearing. The gift of a girdle [belt] is a token of the greatest confidence and affection, and is highly prized.[1]

This took place just after David had killed the giant Goliath. David was quickly rising in prominence in Israel. Jonathan, instead of harboring jealousy and bitterness as his father Saul would come to do, recognized David's courage and faith in God. He was drawn to David and pledged his loyalty to him. In Jonathan, we see three characteristics of a loyal friend.

He Defends His Friend

A fair-weather friend can be kind to your face, but critical of you behind your back when it is to his advantage. It can be disillusioning. But there is no backstabbing, no two-facedness, from a loyal friend.

Saul told his son Jonathan and all the attendants to kill David. But Jonathan was very fond of David and warned him. . . .

Jonathan spoke well of David to Saul his father and said to him, "Let not the king do wrong to his servant David; he has not wronged you, and what he has done has benefited you greatly" (1 Samuel 19:1-4).

Proverbs 17:17 says, "A friend loves at all times, and a brother is born for adversity." In the midst of adversity, Jonathan was loyal to David. Even though it put himself at risk, he defended his friend.

He Knows How to Keep a Secret

Though Jonathan knew the whereabouts of David, he refused to tell his jealous father Saul. A loyal friend can keep a secret.

I heard about four Christian men who decided they would establish an accountability group. They knew they needed friendship and they needed to be accountable to one another. In their first meeting they said, "Let's share some of our weaknesses. The Bible says we should confess our faults to one another."

One man said, "I have to be honest, I have been embezzling money from my company."

After a long pause another said, "I'm ashamed to admit it, but I have not always been faithful to my wife."

A third said, "Well, while we're dumping the facts, I've had a secret drinking problem for years."

The fourth stood up and said, "Gentlemen, I have battled a problem all of my life. My problem is gossip—and I can't wait to get out of this meeting!"

Some people think a secret is something you tell only one person at a time! Others feel there is a statute of limitations on secrets: a secret can be told after two years or if you are more than 500 miles away. But Proverbs 16:28 says, "A perverse man stirs up dissension, and a gossip separates close friends."

A loyal friend knows how to keep his mouth shut and show restraint when it comes to intimate knowledge. A loyal friend is someone who knows enough to ruin you, but never will.

He Can Confront His Friend With the Truth

The world will flatter you to your face and then ridicule you behind your back. Loyal friends tell one another the truth. "He who rebukes a man will in the end gain more favor than he who has a flattering tongue" (Proverbs 28:23).

David and Jonathan were honest with one another. First Samuel 20 records a disagreement they had over Saul's attitude toward David:

> Then David fled from Naioth at Ramah and went to Jonathan and asked, "What have I done? What is my crime? How have I wronged your father, that he is trying to take my life?"

"Never!" Jonathan replied. "You are not going to die! Look, my father doesn't do anything, great or small, without confiding in me. Why would he hide this from me? It's not so!" (1 Samuel 20:1, 2).

Jonathan loved David, but he was blind to his father's hatred of David. But David gently persuaded Jonathan to speak with his father to discover what Saul's attitude truly was toward David. Jonathan learned that David was right; Saul wanted to kill him. In fact, Saul nearly killed Jonathan because he stood up for David. When Jonathan returned to David with the news, they wept together and David fled for his life.

Jonathan said to David, "Go in peace, for we have sworn friendship with each other in the name of the Lord" (1 Samuel 20:42).

Proverbs 27: 5, 6 reads, "Better is open rebuke than hidden love. Wounds of a friend can be trusted, but an enemy multiplies kisses." Occasionally, loyal friends must tell us the truth about our spiritual blind spots, even when it hurts. If you saw me getting ready to light a match in the presence of gasoline fumes, you would not be a faithful friend unless you tried to stop me, even if you had to be abrupt.

If you have a friend who has a drinking problem or is cheating on his wife or is drifting away from the church, you are not being loyal if you stand by and let it happen because you don't want to offend him or endanger the relationship. If you have a child that is heading toward disaster, no matter how old he is, it would be less than loving for you to let him destroy his life without saying a word.

However, this is where tact comes in. Someone said that tact is "the ability to make your point without making an enemy." The object is not simply to prove you know everything; you want to win over your child or your friend. You must speak the truth in love. Confront gently and tactfully.

"Brothers, if someone is caught in a sin, you who are spiritual restore should him *gently*" (Galatians 6:1, emphasis added).

Friends Are Unselfish

"An unfriendly man pursues selfish ends; he defies all sound judgment" (Proverbs 18:1).

I cringe when I hear engaged couples claim that their marriage is going to be "fifty-fifty." They think everything is going to be divided up equally. Such a marriage does not exist, at least not for long. A successful marriage is not one that is divided up "fifty-fifty," but one in which both the man and the woman decide to give up one hundred percent of themselves for the other. The same is true for successful friendships. David and Jonathan gave up of themselves, even risking their lives for one another.

Love is patient, love is kind. It does not envy, it does not boast, it is not proud. It is not rude, it is not self-seeking, it is not easily angered, it keeps no record of wrongs. Love does not delight in evil but rejoices with the truth. It always protects, always trusts, always hopes, always perseveres. Love never fails (1 Corinthians 13:4-8).

An Unselfish Friend Sacrifices Personal Interests

An unselfish friend does not have to be in the limelight. He is willing to sacrifice time, money, glory, and his own desires for the benefit of others.

It takes an unselfish parent to say to his grown children, "Maybe it would be better if you stayed at home and started your own traditions on Christmas Day."

It takes an unselfish parent to agree to baby-sit the grandkids without much warning when their parents are in a bind.

Only an unselfish parent can smile and say, "That's OK; we'll do it another time," when the children turn down a request for dinner together.

An Unselfish Friend Is Not Possessive

Paul mentioned in 1 Corinthians 13:4 that loves does not envy. An unselfish friend does not insist that he be the only friend. He is not jealous when others demand the friend's time.

An unselfish parent does not get offended when the child decides to go to college out of town or decides to take a job out of the state. It takes unselfishness for the parents to understand that, after the wedding, their son must consider his wife a higher priority than his parents. It takes unselfishness for the parents to enjoy the company of their grown children without complaining that they don't visit often enough.

An Unselfish Friend Is Sensitive to Changing Moods

"Like one who takes away a garment on a cold day, or like vinegar poured on soda, is one who sings songs to a heavy heart" (Proverbs 25:20).

Everyone has ups and downs. The unselfish person does not demand that his friend share his mood. The Bible commands us to rejoice with those who rejoice and weep with those who weep (Romans 12:15). Friends are sensitive to the fluctuating moods of others and can respond accordingly.

Sometimes it can be more difficult to rejoice with those who rejoice, even if it is your children. Can you still rejoice with your child if he finds a job that makes more money than yours, or if he moves into a nicer home, or if she becomes more attractive, or seems more fulfilled in her marriage? It is not always easy to rejoice with those who rejoice.

But neither is it easy to mourn with those who mourn. We all hate to see our children suffer, and we naturally want to see them cheer up. Sometimes they may be hurting over something that seems trivial to you, or something that you may have warned them about and they could have avoided. It is hard not to say, "I told you so," or, "Just pick yourself up and go on." But our children need friends who will weep with them when they weep.

Thank you for being a friend to me
When needing someone there,
My failing hopes to bolster,
My secret fears to share.

Thank you for being so good to me
When it was hard to know
The wisest course to follow,
What to do and where to go.

Thank you for giving me
Confidence when I had lost my way,
Speaking the word that led me
Through the tunnel of the day.

Thank you for all you did and said
To ease the weight for me,
Never intruding, but there in the background,
Helping quietly.

Thank you not only for sympathy
In times of grief and stress,
But for all you have meant to me
In terms of happiness.

Many a lovely day we've known
And many a laugh we've had.
Thank you for being the kind of friend
Who shares the good and bad.

—Patience Strong

Friends Are Forgiving

King Saul's jealousy of David continued to grow. Saul and his army pursued David and his band of men several times, attempting to arrest and kill David. But David continued to escape, and graciously passed up two chances to kill King Saul himself. The last chapter of 1 Samuel records that both Jonathan and Saul died in a battle with the Philistines. Shortly afterwards David was anointed king of Judah.

Traditionally, the new king would execute the descendants of the previous king so that there would be no future rivalry between the two families. The people assumed David would do the same. So when the news about the death of Jonathan and Saul reached the palace, panic broke out.

Jonathan had a five-year-old son named Mephibosheth. Mephibosheth's nurse picked him up to flee the city, probably fearing that both the Philistines and the new king would be out to get Mephibosheth. As she fled, she dropped him, and Mephibosheth became crippled for life. (See 2 Samuel 4:4.)

Several years later, King David decided to inquire about the living descendants of Saul. He discovered that Mephibosheth was still alive and he sent for him. Mephibosheth came, fearing for his life, and bowed before the King of Israel.

But David reassured Mephibosheth that he meant him no harm. Instead, the king meant to show him kindness for the sake of his devoted friend Jonathan. David restored to

Mephibosheth all the land that had belonged to Saul and made provision for him to eat at the king's table (2 Samuel 9:7, 8).

Such treatment to a member of the previous dynasty was unheard of. A gracious new king might allow the potential rival to live, but would often banish him to live in exile, removed from the capital city where he might cause trouble. David showed total forgiveness and restored Mephibosheth to the status of a prince. David's love for Jonathan resulted in his forgiveness of King Saul, not only while Saul was alive, but even long after his death.

Christian friends must be willing to forgive. No friend is perfect. Sometimes friends are selfish; sometimes they hurt you without even knowing it. Sometimes we exaggerate problems or imagine offenses that don't even exist. But real love "keeps no record of wrongs" (1 Corinthians 13:5). Learn to forgive quickly.

"He who covers over an offense promotes love, but whoever repeats the matter separates close friends" (Proverbs 17:9).

I know a man who loaned a close friend fifty dollars. When the borrower failed to repay the loan, it irritated the man so much that he began backing away from the relationship and lost a friend. If it bothered him that much, he should have been honest enough to confront his friend. Maybe the friend forgot or was embarrassed to bring it up. But even better, he should have forgiven the debt. No friendship is worth being lost over fifty dollars.

David Augsburger tells of a man who could have ended up much the same, but he decided to forgive instead. For many years there had been a barrier between this man and his wife, a distance he could neither understand nor close. It spoiled their relationship and scarred their children. Then, finally, after ten years of silence, she told him the truth: there had been an affair, an affair with his best friend!

"Oooh, but I'm going to get him," he said to himself, again and again. "I'll burn him in front of his wife. She's a proud one. When she hears she'll make it miserable for him. I'll rub him in the dirt until he can't even look up to a worm." . . .

"Why I went to church that morning, I'll never know," he told me later. "Something in me I could not hear must have been crying out for help. I slipped quietly into the door. And there he stood. His hand out, the same old smile saying his saccharin hello. . . .

"'I'll never forgive that man,' I'd vowed again and again. . . . 'He'll pay for every painful moment I've suffered through ten miserable years.' . . .

"Then, with a sob in my soul, my hand came out and gripped his. I took the hand of the man who'd betrayed everything I loved. The man who'd ruined my whole life for a few moments' passion. And for the first time in my life, I knew what it was to forgive. For the first time I felt the tremendous sense of freedom, of liberty, of lighter-than-air release as the unbearable weight of bitterness washed out of me. And I was free. Free to forgive. Free to live again!

"And that new freedom not only gave me the strength to go on; it gave me the resources to love my way through that barrier between my wife and me too. When I told her 'I forgive you! I accept you just as I did that day we pledged to love and cherish until death,' then healing began its slow change."[2]

We shouldn't forget that there are occasions when sin must be confronted. Jesus said in Matthew 18:15, "If your brother sins against you, go and show him his fault just between the two of you. If he listens to you, you have won your brother over." We are being less than loving when we do not confront continual or rebellious sin in the lives of our Christian friends. The man above would have been foolish to forgive his friend and allow the affair to continue![3]

Every relationship experiences times of hurt feelings, disappointments, and wrongs suffered. It is impossible for two human beings to have a close relationship without ever experiencing some friction. That is especially true with families, where our closeness often makes us too comfortable with one another, causing us to behave toward one another differently than we would ever behave toward someone outside the family.

When your children hurt your feelings, as they certainly will do occasionally, learn to forgive quickly. It is difficult for your child to love you as much as you love your child, no matter how old the child becomes. You carried her in your womb. You watched him grow up. You changed their diapers and heard them speak their first words. You have a special bond with them that they will never fully comprehend. Don't expect them to. Forgive them and love them anyway. Learn to be a friend when they need one, and back off when they don't.

Someday they will have children of their own, and then perhaps they will begin to understand.

There is no way that we could ever love Jesus as much as he loves us. But in the same way that he loves and forgives us, he commands us to love and forgive others (Matthew 6:12-14).

Be kind and compassionate to one another, forgiving each other, just as in Christ God forgave you (Ephesians 4:32).

For the most part, when a child grows older, his attitude toward his parents changes dramatically for the better. I am now fifty years old and my two sons are grown. I have often told them that I enjoy them much more now than when they were younger. My sons and I enjoy going to ball games together, golfing together, and fellowshiping around the meal table together. They have both married wonderful Christian women, and I love my daughters-in-law. You aren't supposed to spoil your kids, but I think it's okay to spoil their spouses!

My son paid me a great compliment a couple years ago when he introduced me at a gathering where I was to speak. He introduced me not just as his father, but also as his friend. That is the ultimate goal of parenting. The dangers of trying to be the child's "buddy" too early have already been noted. But what a joyous time of life is missed—for both the parents and the child—if that friendship does not develop when the child reaches maturity. It is truly a blessing when your adult child calls you friend.

---

[1]James Freeman, *Manners and Customs of the Bible*, Bridge Publishing, Inc. 1972.

[2]David Augsburger, *Seventy Times Seven: The Freedom of Forgiveness* (Chicago: Moody, 1970), pp. 9-12.

[3]For more information on confronting sin, let me recommend two excellent books: James Dobson's *Love Must Be Tough*, written especially for individuals whose family members are caught up in a continual sin; and Don Baker's *Beyond Forgiveness*, written primarily for church leaders about church discipline.

CHAPTER EIGHT

Encourage Evangelism

Naaman's Servant

2 Kings 5

In the fifth chapter of 2 Kings, during the ministry of the great prophet Elisha, there is a story about a pagan military leader and a Jewish slave girl that gives us insight into how to teach our children to be evangelists for Christ.

> Now Naaman was commander of the army of the king of Aram. He was a great man in the sight of his master and highly regarded, because through him the Lord had given victory to Aram. He was a valiant soldier, but he had leprosy (2 Kings 5:1).

Aram and Israel were enemies but had recently made a shaky peace treaty. Throughout this time of supposed peace, there were still occasional skirmishes along the borders of the two countries. During one of the skirmishes, a young Israelite girl was taken captive and became a servant to Naaman's wife (2 Kings 5:2).

It must have been difficult to be a slave. This young girl had been kidnapped from her home and the prospects of ever returning looked slim. She was in a foreign country, among strangers who forced her to work for nothing but her food. Most of us would have turned bitter. We would have hoped and prayed for revenge. We would have secretly gained pleasure when our master suffered harm.

But not this girl. Though she was treated like property, she believed in the worth of every person—even her mistress and her mistress's leprous husband.

> She said to her mistress, "If only my master would see the prophet who is in Samaria! He would cure him of his leprosy" (2 Kings 5:3).

Elisha was known as a miracle worker. It is doubtful that the young girl had ever actually met him, but she had certainly heard the stories. He had parted the Jordan River and raised a young boy from the dead. He had fed one hundred people with just a few loaves of bread. He had inherited the power to do miracles from his predecessor Elijah, who had also been famous in Israel. The young slave girl knew Elisha could heal her master Naaman. And for some reason, she wanted to see him healed.

For some reason, Naaman listened. Upon the advice of his servant girl, Naaman headed for Israel with an entourage of soldiers and bodyguards, a letter from the King of Aram, and horses and chariots loaded down with gifts.

> So Naaman went with his horses and chariots and stopped at the door of Elisha's house. Elisha sent a messenger to say to him, "Go, wash yourself seven times in the Jordan, and your flesh will be restored and you will be cleansed" (2 Kings 5:9, 10).

This was not exactly a hero's welcome. Naaman was used to fanfares, cheering crowds, and autograph seekers. He was a proud warrior who commanded hundreds of soldiers. It was humbling enough to have this wretched disease that literally ate away at his flesh. It was humbling enough to travel for miles out of desperation, on the advice of a slave girl, to visit a faith healer. Then the prophet did not even come to the door to greet him! Naaman must have felt insulted in front of his men.

The prophet then sent him a message that was even more humbling: "If you want to be healed, go dip yourself in the Jordan River—the muddy Jordan River—seven times."

Naaman expected the prophet to come out, slap him on the forehead and say, "Be healed!" He had hoped there would be reporters and cameramen present to record the great event. But the prophet didn't even come out to greet him. Naaman was furious.

> Naaman went away angry and said, "I thought that he would surely come out to me and stand and call on the name of the Lord his God, wave his hand over the spot and cure me of my leprosy. Are not Abana and Pharpar, the rivers of Damascus, better than any of the waters of Israel? Couldn't I wash in them and be cleansed?" So he turned and went off in a rage (2 Kings 5:11, 12).

Elisha knew Naaman needed more than just healing from his leprosy. He needed a lesson in humility, too. But let's not be too hard on Naaman. None of us likes to be treated as if we're not important. And the more famous you are, the more humbling it can be to discover that some people still don't think you are very significant.

Christian Herter, former governor of Massachusetts, normally a very unassuming man, was once at a picnic supper at the end of a long day in which he had been forced to skip breakfast and lunch. When he went through the line, the lady passing out the chicken gave him only one small piece of chicken. He said, politely, "Ma'am, may I have another piece of chicken?"

She said, "No. One per person."

He said, "Ma'am, I am really hungry and I haven't eaten all day. May I please have another piece of chicken?"

She said, "No. One piece per person."

He said, "Ma'am, do you know who I am? I'm the governor of this state."

She said, "Do you know who I am? I'm the lady who passes out the chicken. Now move along!"

Naaman felt humiliated by Elisha's treatment, and he refused to head toward the Jordan River. But as they were leaving, some wise bodyguards changed his mind.

> Naaman's servants went to him and said, "My father, if the prophet had told you to do some great thing, would you not have done it? How much more, then, when he tells you, 'Wash and be cleansed'!" (2 Kings 5:13).

Naaman decided it was worth a try, so they headed toward the Jordan River. There Naaman, in front of all of his servants, took off the coat with its general's stars and stripes, stripped down, and waded out into the muddy Jordan River. He did just what Elisha had told him to do, dipping himself seven times in the Jordan River. "And his flesh was restored and became clean like that of a young boy" (2 Kings 5:14).

About the worst skin ailment I've ever had is poison ivy. It can't compare to leprosy, but it sure is miserable. Can you imagine what it would be like to have a skin ailment that is life-threatening, that causes people to gawk at you when they see you, that causes excruciating pain and itching and threatens to make your limbs literally fall off—and then suddenly to be healed? No longer would you have to suffer the pain and the itching. No longer would you be forced to endure the stares of others. No longer would you be looking death in the face. Naaman had to have come out of the water whooping and hollering!

> Then Naaman and all his attendants went back to the man of God. He stood before him and said, "Now I know that there is no God in all the world except in Israel"(2 Kings 5:15).

A pagan general had come to know the one true and living God because of the testimony of a young slave girl. Perhaps the greatest thing that you can do for your children, besides leading them to Christ, is to encourage them to become evangelists—faithful witnesses for Christ wherever God may lead them.

Notice some truths about this slave girl that will help us encourage evangelism in our children.

She Was Sensitive to Her Master's Need

You would think she would be tempted to take pleasure in the pain her master was experiencing. Yet, this young Hebrew girl cared about those who had cared so little about her. She did not bury herself in her own suffering or selfishly take pleasure in others' pain.

We are surrounded by hurting people. We all know people experiencing the pains of broken homes, physical illnesses, loneliness, and abuse. One old preacher told his young apprentice, "Son, whenever you preach, remember that there is a broken heart in every pew."

Jesus was great at sensing the needs of people. We often read that he "felt compassion" for those he saw. He wanted to heal the leper, to forgive the sinner, to comfort the bereaved, and to lead the lost.

But feeling compassion for people is not something that comes naturally to most of us. If we are not careful, we can miss the hurts people are feeling and steamroll right past them. It is especially difficult for children to notice hurting people. Children can be cruel to suffering people. Therefore, we must work to develop in them a compassion for the hurting.

My son Rusty says it helped him to empathize with those who are handicapped when he participated in what was called a "Deeper Life Week" at White Mills Christian Camp several years ago. They spent a day learning what it was like to have different handicaps. Some wore blindfolds to learn what it was like to be blind. Some pretended to be lame and had to be wheeled around in wheelchairs. Rusty became a deaf person for a day. With cotton balls in his ears and bandages around his head to insure he could not hear, he tried his best to play softball, to listen to instructions at meals, and to communicate with friends. He could still play softball, but communication was difficult. He felt isolated. Someone said that being blind cuts you off from things, but being deaf cuts you off from people. Rusty now can empathize with those who cannot hear. Maybe that's the reason he was especially moved recently when we witnessed a deaf man in our church use sign language to confess his faith in Christ before he was baptized.

Do not try to protect your children from people who are hurting or who have disabilities. Introduce them to people with physical handicaps. Take them with you to the hospital to visit a friend who is ill. I think it is important when they are old enough that they attend funerals and understand the hurt and loneliness that losing a loved one brings to family and friends. Take your children with you to give gifts to a poor family at Christmas, or to visit someone in prison. Jesus said that the ones whom he would call his followers in Heaven would be the ones who took care of the "least of these," who visited the sick and those in prison, and who took care of those in need (Matthew 25:31-46).

She Spoke Up With Courage and Clarity

The girl in this story was a slave girl. She could have been viewed as disrespectful when she spoke up with her suggestion that Naaman visit an Israelite prophet. And think of what would have happened if she had been wrong about Elisha and he could not heal Naaman of his leprosy! The servant girl would have been the brunt of Naaman's anger. What faith and courage she expressed!

Naaman was skeptical, but she told him anyway. Her faith was not wavering. She pulled no punches. She did not say, "I have an idea that might work—but I can't make any promises." She said, "I know exactly what you need to do."

Most of us would not be that bold in speaking with our bosses, or anyone else whom we respected. We often see that people are hurting and know they need the Lord but do not have the courage to speak up as this servant girl did.

Children tend to have difficulty communicating clearly with adults at any time. It is something they must be trained to do. Children must be trained to look another person in the eye and say "thank you" when complimented, or to respond without hiding behind Mom when a stranger wants to greet them, or to speak up without mumbling and to speak with a smile.

Teaching children to communicate clearly may seem like a small thing, but without those skills, it will be difficult for them to learn to communicate the important truths of life to those who are hurting. Simply learning to empathize with the hurting will not help anyone. We must be able to communicate our empathy to them, and, if it is a spiritual hurting, we must be able to tell them how they can be healed.

The servant girl didn't need lessons in theology to become a great evangelist. I doubt that her understanding of theological truths was really that deep. She simply had faith in God, felt empathy for a hurting human being, and courageously communicated the solution.

She Had Previously Gained Credibility

If the servant girl had not been a good worker, then Naaman would not have listened to her suggestion. If she had been lazy and had done only that which was required of her, or if she had been a complainer, Naaman wouldn't have trusted her and put his ego on the line. This servant girl had gained credibility with Naaman and his wife. She must have been full of honesty and integrity, or she would not have been so trusted.

Children need to be taught that there are several reasons we should always be honest. The first is that God has commanded us to be truthful. He sees us at all times and knows whether we are now telling the truth or living a double life.

Another reason for integrity is that your life will be more peaceful and fulfilling if you are not always worried about covering up your lies.

But children should also be taught that living an honest life helps them gain credibility with others. If you are to influence other people for good, and if you are to be an evangelist for Christ, then you must be an honest person in the smaller issues of life. People will trust you when you give them advice that is life-changing only if they have learned they can always trust you to tell the truth. They have to know you are a person who will keep your promises, tell the whole truth, and live an authentic life.

Keep Your Promises

An honest person keeps his word. If he says he will get the job done on Tuesday, the job is done on Tuesday. If she says she will spend only twenty dollars, she spends no more than twenty dollars. If he says he will be home by six o'clock, he is home by six.

Children should be taught that to break a promise is almost always less than honest. Occasionally, there are unforeseen and uncontrollable circumstances that arise. But otherwise, if you say you will do your chores before supper and they are not done, then you have not told the truth. If you say you will be in by eleven o'clock from your date and you come home at 11:15, then you have not been honest. You have broken the trust others had in your word and you have lost credibility. Sometimes that credibility is hard to gain back.

Tell the Whole Truth

We love to master in half-truths. A woman made a cake for a preacher and his family, but it was so bad they had to throw it away. A few weeks later the woman asked the preacher how the family had liked the cake. He replied, "Well, cake like that just doesn't last long around our house!"

It is good to show tact and to be kind to people, but to leave out part of the facts so that someone believes something you know not to be true is to tell a lie. Let's say a mother asks her teenager where he went last night, and he says, "I went over to my friend Johnny's." But suppose he went someplace else first—someplace he was not supposed to go—and then he went to Johnny's. He is telling a partial truth: he did go to Johnny's. But he is not telling the whole truth. He is deliberately leaving out part of the story to make Mom believe something he knows not to be true. He is lying! Children need to be taught that such behavior is dishonest and unacceptable.

Live an Authentic Life

It is probably impossible to teach children how to live an authentic life unless you are modeling it for them. Children learn how to be dishonest when their parents or people they respect live two different lives. If you are kind to everyone except the members of your own family, that is not authentic. Your children will not only resent your being unkind, they will also learn how to live a double life. If you have habits at home that you try to conceal at church, your children will learn that appearances are more important than truth. They'll learn how to live a double life.

But if you are the same at home as you are at church or around others, your children will learn to model authenticity. If you practice what you preach by guarding your own tongue when you get angry, by praying at meals and before bed just as you do at church, and by showing kindness to your spouse and children as you show kindness to others, then your children will instinctively understand the importance of living the same way all the time. In fact, when they get older, they'll be shocked by those who can pretend to be Christians and are living like the world behind the scenes. You will hear them say they can't understand how such people can live with themselves.

The servant girl was like that. We don't know who her parents were, but they had taught her to be authentic. They had taught her that her testimony for God would be enhanced if she did the simple things right—show up to work on time, do a good job, be kind to people all the time, keep your temper under control, don't talk behind others' backs. She had gained credibility by her authentic life.

Make it your ambition to lead a quiet life, to mind your own business and to work with your hands, just as we told you, so that your daily life may win the respect of outsiders and so that you will not be dependent on anybody (1 Thessalonians 4:11, 12).

She Witnessed Positive Results

Can you imagine the joy the servant girl felt when Naaman came home cleansed of his leprosy? Even though she was a slave, can't you picture Naaman giving that little girl a big bear hug? I'll bet the relationship between the servant girl and her masters changed dramatically after that event!

Still, we cannot assume that much changed in the life of this servant girl after Naaman returned. We do not read that Naaman let her go and granted her freedom, allowing her to return to her homeland. We do not read that he and his wife adopted her into their family and treated her like one of their own daughters. We don't even discover the girl's name.

Often, the purest evangelism receives no reward here on this earth. The evangelist goes unnoticed as the angels rejoice over the repenting sinner.

Steve Brown tells of a wonderful compliment he received once. A woman came to him with a friend of hers that she wanted to introduce. She said to her friend, "This is the preacher I have been telling you about. He has been instrumental in bringing me to Christ. Preacher, what's your name again?" Our job is to present Christ to people, not to make a name for ourselves.

Once when Lloyd Olgilvie was the featured speaker at a banquet, the man who was to introduce the speaker stood and said, "Today, you will meet someone who is known literally around the world. He has been instrumental in changing thousands of lives. He has been called a great teacher and a man of compassion. His name is Jesus Christ, and here is Lloyd Olgilvie to talk about him."

The best evangelists do not care about recognition. They only want to witness the results that come from sharing the message.

We need to teach our kids that they don't have to be great scholars to witness positive results in evangelism. Somebody said that evangelism is one beggar telling another beggar where he can find bread. Ninety-five percent of the evangelism I witness is a result of someone's inviting a friend or relative to come to church. Evangelism does not require a Bible college degree—just a desire to help those in need. The servant girl had discovered that truth; as a result, she succeeded in helping to change Naaman's life.

Bob Dabney of our church decided a couple of years ago that he was going to trace someone's spiritual family tree. He saw General Chager, an army officer stationed at Fort Knox. "General Chager," he said, "How did you start coming to this church?"

"My brother-in-law, Jim Hatfield, invited me to come," General Chager said.

Bob Dabney then asked Jim Hatfield how he began attending Southeast Christian Church. "I knew Johnny Sampson in high school," Jim said, "and he was kind of a 'rounder.' Then I met him a couple of years ago, and his life had turned around. He told me what had happened to him and invited me to come to church with him."

Johnny Sampson was asked the same question. He said, "I was working out at the fitness center, and George Fields was riding the stationary bicycle next to mine. We began talking about families, and I told him about how I was struggling with raising my teenagers. He told me how much of a difference going to church had made on his family, and he invited me to Southeast."

George Fields said, "We had been attending a church where we did not feel we were being fed the Word of God. Our children were enrolled at Christian Academy of Louisville with Darryl and Betty Weaver's kids. They asked us to come to church with them."

The Weavers are in real estate. They said they had met Bob and Mary Helen Vaughn through their business. Bob and Mary Helen had invited them to come to church with them.

Bob Dabney continued his search, asking Bob and Mary Helen how they came to Southeast. "Mary Helen was teaching music at the school where Junior Wortham was the principal," Bob said. "Junior invited her to come to hear a concert by the Master's Men choir."

Junior Wortham said, "One of the teachers at my school was Elizabeth Harvin. She had been inviting me for months to come to her little church that was growing and doing well. I finally came and have been coming ever since."

How did Elizabeth Harvin begin coming to Southeast Christian Church? She said, "In 1962, I was driving down Hikes Lane one Sunday morning, and I saw a sign that said, 'Southeast Christian Church,' so I pulled in!"

It is amazing to think of the lives that were changed for eternity because one lady had the courage to invite her principal to come to her church. Teach your children about the eternal rewards that can come when we sympathize with the hurting and clearly tell them how to find healing for their souls.

CHAPTER NINE

Foster Faithfulness

Joash

2 Kings 11, 12; 2 Chronicles 23, 24

The story of Joash in the Old Testament has all the necessary ingredients for an excellent movie plot. War, treason, a wicked stepmother, a young prince kidnapped for his own good—all these are subplots in the story of Joash. The climax comes when the young prince becomes king of the nation of Judah when he is just seven years old!

During the time of the divided kingdoms of Israel and Judah, two wicked kings—Joram, the son of Ahab and king of Israel, and Ahaziah, the king of Judah—were together on a rare occasion when civil war broke out in the kingdom of Israel. A man named Jehu had been anointed by God to become the next king of Israel, and had been commissioned by God to wipe out all the descendants of the evil king Ahab. Jehu's men killed both kings in the battle.

The mother of Ahaziah, the king of Judah, was a wicked woman named Athaliah, a niece of Ahab. When she heard her son had died, she tried to take over the kingdom. But in order to take over the throne, she had to kill all the sons of Ahaziah. She began brutally murdering her own grandchildren!

But God providentially spared one young prince, a son of Ahaziah named Joash. When Joash is first introduced, in 2 Kings 11, he is only a baby. His grandmother Athaliah is coming to kill all of the young sons of Ahaziah so she can take over the kingdom herself. But Joash had a brave aunt, Jehosheba, who saved his life. Apparently a stepdaughter of the wicked queen, Jehosheba stole Joash away from the royal princes just as all the sons of Ahaziah were about to be murdered. She was the wife of the priest Jehoiada, so she smuggled him to the temple and hid him from her wicked stepmother. There Joash remained hidden for six years while his grandmother Athaliah ruled with an iron fist (2 Kings 11:2, 3).

When Joash was seven years old, Jehoiada secured the support of the army and brought Joash out into the open for the first time, declaring him to be the rightful king of Judah. The army protected Joash, the people supported him, and the wicked queen Athaliah was put to death.

> The king then took his place on the royal throne, and all the people of the land rejoiced. And the city was quiet, because Athaliah had been slain with the sword at the palace (2 Kings 11:19, 20).

Joash was used by God from the time he was an infant. He literally grew up in the temple and continued to be faithful to God throughout much of his adult life.

Tragically, near the end of his life, Joash rejected God. He shows that growing up in the church is no guarantee that you will remain faithful to God throughout your life. Though we are reminded that every child must someday take responsibility for his own actions, by studying the story of Joash, we can gain insight into how to encourage faithfulness in our own children.

He Was Protected

The wicked queen Athaliah was out to destroy Joash, but Aunt Jehosheba stole him and protected him from this terrible adversary. Our children also have an adversary who wants to destroy them. Paul commanded:

> Be strong in the Lord and in his mighty power. Put on the full armor of God so that you can take your stand against the devil's schemes. For our struggle is not against flesh and blood, but against the rulers, against the authorities, against the powers of this dark world and against the spiritual forces of evil in the heavenly realms. Therefore put on the full armor of God, so that when

day of evil comes, you may be able to stand your ground, and after you have done everything, to stand (Ephesians 6:10-13).

Satan is out to kill our children, both physically and spiritually. He wants to enslave children into drugs, promiscuity, alcoholism, pornography, and anything else that will destroy them. We are waging a spiritual battle, and we must do all we can to protect our children.

The United States Surgeon General, Joycelyn Elders, has stated publicly, "We need to speak out to tell people that sex is good; sex is wonderful. It's a normal part and a healthy part of our being, whether it is homosexual or heterosexual."

The philosophies of the adversary are promoted as normal today, making it even more difficult for us to protect our children. But regardless of how many people believe them, the enemy's philosophies are still lies. Sex *is* good, but only within the bonds of marriage. Outside of those bonds, it causes heartache, broken families, disease, broken relationships, distrust, and guilt.

Jesus said,

[The devil] was a murderer from the beginning, not holding to the truth, for there is no truth in him. When he lies, he speaks his native language, for he is a liar and the father of lies. Yet because I tell the truth, you do not believe me! (John 8:44, 45).

To protect our children from Satan's deadly schemes, we must be alert, creative, and sometimes radical in our measures. Paul said, "Be strong in the Lord and in his mighty power" (Ephesians 6:10).

Some parents in our church are choosing to have no television sets in their homes because of the negative influence television can have on young minds. One family does not allow the children to watch television without permission, and then only rarely. Some might say that is eccentric, but it might be the parents' way of temporarily hiding the children from the adversary as Jehosheba hid Joash. If you have watched television with a discerning eye lately, you can easily understand why parents today might choose to take such measures!

Thousands of parents across America have chosen to educate their children at home. Those children have proven to perform better at academic achievement tests than their public-school counterparts. They also have a greater sense of bonding with the parents who have spent so much time with them. In most cases, Christian values are taught in those home schools, and we must applaud them. The Bible clearly declares it to be the parents' responsibility to educate their children (Deuteronomy 6:6-8).

Many parents are choosing Christian schools. Others are refusing to enroll their child in any public school class without first having a session with the teacher to discover the teacher's beliefs and philosophies.

No loving parent would trust a four-year-old child to a baby-sitter without first checking out the baby-sitter's credentials. Is she trustworthy? Has he ever been around small children before? Do others see her as a person of good character and a kind spirit? If a parent would ask these things of a baby-sitter for a four-year-old, doesn't it seem reasonable for parents to question the credentials and beliefs of those with whom they will be entrusting the mind of their six-year-old child, or even their thirteen- or fourteen-year-old adolescent?

Many Christian parents are taking classes on child-rearing, like Gary and Anne Marie Ezzo's course, *Growing Kids God's Way*. In the Ezzos' course, parents are taught to discipline their children at a young age and to train them to be submissive to authority and to respect adults. Some would say that is too strict. It certainly is contrary to the world's philosophy of child-rearing. But in today's culture, parents must often reject the world's philosophy of child-rearing. That philosophy is based on the belief that children should be able to live as they please with no moral bounds. Christians believe that God gave us commands—moral absolutes—that we are to follow. We will save our children much harm if we teach them to follow those commands. We are strict by the world's standards because we love our children and desire to protect them.

He Was Respected

Joash was also respected at a young age, which had to be a challenge for those trying to rear this young prince. He became king of Judah when he was seven years old (2 Kings 11:21).

We tend to think people in the past weren't as smart as people are today. After all, we reason, they didn't have computers, televisions, telephones, or even electricity. How could they have been as smart as we are? Yet there is no real evidence to believe we have become smarter. To the contrary, there have been many times in the past when people achieved extraordinary success at very young ages. Take, for example, some of the founding fathers of America:

Fischer Ames entered Harvard when he was only twelve years old.

John Trumble read through the Bible at age four. When he was six years old, he won a Greek contest against a local minister. He proceeded to pass the entrance exam to Yale at age seven!

John Quincy Adams became America's diplomat to Russia when he was fourteen years old. How many fourteen-year-olds do you know who could take on that kind of responsibility today?[1]

The book of Proverbs tells us that the fear of the Lord is the beginning of knowledge and wisdom. At age seven, Joash may not have had the years of experience most think is needed for such a high office, but the Lord saw fit to make Joash king because he had that foundation for wisdom: He feared and obeyed God. He was an exceptional child.

I have two older sisters who were very high achievers academically. Rosanne was valedictorian of her graduating class at our high school, and Carolyn was the salutatorian of her graduating class. When I came along, I didn't quite measure up to the academic standards of my older sisters. The teachers would ask me, "Are you sure you're Rosanne Russell's brother?"

It is not always easy to raise a child who is exceptional. Others might resent him or be envious. She might have difficulty being patient with kids her own age who aren't as smart. It can be a challenge to teach humility, patience and tolerance of those who are different. But with God's help, those who surrounded Joash were successful in teaching this exceptional child to be faithful to his God.

He Was Faithful

There are two insights into the reign of Joash as king that reveal his continued faithfulness to God. First, he continued to maintain a teachable spirit.

Joash did what was right in the eyes of the Lord all the years Jehoiada the priest instructed him (2 Kings 12:2).

The more intelligent and talented you are, the more tempting it can be for you to become proud and unteachable. Joash did not fall to that temptation. He continued to learn at the feet of the priest throughout much of his reign as king.

The second insight into Joash's life involves his desire to repair the temple. The preceding kings had cared little about the state of the temple, which is significant because it was seen as the actual dwelling place of God. To be apathetic about the temple was to be apathetic about God. Athaliah had done even worse, abusing and profaning the temple with idol worship (2 Chronicles 24:7).

Joash commanded the priests to repair the temple. He wanted the temple to be given the respect it deserved as the house of God. But the priests were slow to follow his commands, so Joash literally had to walk into the temple and take control himself. It was something he refused to let go undone.

Yet something happened to the faithfulness of Joash. After the death of his teacher, Jehoiada the priest, Joash began to listen to some other advisers.

After the death of Jehoiada, the officials of Judah came and paid homage to the king, and he listened to them. They abandoned the temple of the Lord, the God of their fathers, and worshiped Asherah poles and idols. Because of their guilt, God's anger came upon Judah and Jerusalem (2 Chronicles 24:17).

Joash's backsliding continued. At his lowest point, he had Zechariah, the son of Jehoiada the priest, killed for preaching out against him. Then, as often happens with ungodly friends, those same officials that had pulled Joash away from God conspired against him and had him assassinated.

Struggles of a Cradle Christian

Growing up in the church (or the temple, in the case of Joash) is no guarantee that you will remain faithful to God. Those who are raised in the church, in contrast with those who come to Christ later in life, face an entirely different set of challenges, doubts, and temptations.

Dave Faust has some excellent insights into what he calls the "Struggles of a Cradle Christian." He mentions several struggles that those who have grown up in the church are bound to experience:

Faust calls the first experience *the doubting dilemma*. He writes, "Cradle Christians commonly experience a time of intense questioning, not only during adolescence, but even into adulthood. 'Is my faith really my own, or is it merely a reflection of my upbringing?'"

The second struggle is *worship burnout*. Faust says,

> By the time cradle Christians graduate from high school, they have sat through hundreds of worship services, Bible classes, youth-group sessions. . . . Spiritual dullness can grow as familiar hymns seem *too* familiar, public prayers seem too predictable, and worship routines seem more habitual than heartfelt."[2]

A third experience is *shattered idealism*. Those who grow up in the church soon learn that the church is not a perfect place. Somewhere on the road to adulthood, the child begins to realize that those who preach messages (or listen to them preached) on Sunday don't always practice them Monday through Saturday. Faust concludes, "Cradle Christians see the church up close and personal. Sometimes it is not pretty."

The next experience Faust discusses is the urge to *top that testimony*. It is common for those who grew up in the church to feel inferior because their testimonies are boring. Most of us "cradle Christians" have no dramatic story to tell about how Christ has changed our lives. Often, we can't even remember what life was like without Christ. When we hear of those who have come from the depths of sin to Christ, and how he has healed them of their addiction to drugs, their promiscuity, or their despair, we can tend to feel inferior.

I am reminded of the man who prayed, "Dear Lord, I've never been drunk or on drugs, I've never been in jail or unfaithful to my wife, but if you can use me in spite of these weaknesses, here I am!"

Though we may be tempted to feel that way at times, Henry Emerson Fosdick wisely said, "There is something better than bringing the prodigal back from the far country, and that is keeping him at home in a right relationship with the father."

The final struggle of the cradle Christian is *self-righteousness.* Cradle Christians tend to have an easier time living the moral life and "being good" than those who did not grow up in the church. The Bible is clear that all have sinned, and those who appear to live a moral life are as lost without Christ as those who have lived the most immoral of lives. But it is still a temptation for the cradle Christian to compare, and to notice the shortcomings of others in areas of temptation that he has never really faced. "The subtle hazard of spiritual smugness must be overcome," Faust says.[3]

Suggestions for Parents

Faust gives four suggestions to the parents of cradle Christians that should help us in raising children who grow up in the church.

First, *communicate.* "Prepare your children for the struggles they will encounter, especially as they approach adolescence."[4] Faust encourages us to talk with our children about current issues in light of the Bible, and to speak openly with them about doubts without appearing shocked when those doubts inevitably come.

Second, *establish contact with non-Christians.* Faust challenges the parents of cradle Christians not to isolate themselves or their children from the unchurched. We should encourage our children to become involved in community events like Little League Baseball, ballet lessons, and neighborhood activities. This will teach cradle Christians not to fear those who are unbelievers, and it will teach them to "speak their language." Jesus did not speak in jargon and hard-to-understand terminology. He spoke so that the common person could understand and respond to his message.

Third, *battle spiritual boredom.* When church services or devotions are boring even to adults, it is easy for a child to get the impression that what is going on is not very important. Be creative, Faust says. Find ways to add spice to your family devotions. Encourage your children to lead in prayer at meals. Experiment with ways to study the Bible together that everyone enjoys. Sometimes the spiritual disciplines are difficult and routine, like practicing for a sport over and over again, and the ultimate purpose of honoring God should not be dependent upon our having fun all the time. But there are creative ways to turn times of drudgery into times that children can enjoy. Doing that will keep their attention and help keep their spiritual fervor alive.

Finally, *strive for authenticity.* Faust says we should work hard to "Fight the good fight of *fake.*" He explains:

> Children sense—and rebel against—any kind of phoniness. Parents must model a genuine, healthy self-image as forgiven children of God. The apostle Paul . . . said, "By the grace of God I am what I am"(1 Corinthians 15:10).[5]

Cradle Christians learn early how to fake Christianity. We learn all the right things to say. We even know the right inflections to make with our voices and the right expressions to put on our faces to make others think we are spiritual. It is important that parents of cradle Christians strive to be authentic. That means we fight the temptation to appear overly pious and spiritual. It also means that we do our best to practice what we preach. Kids will discover we are imperfect, but they should also sense that we are real, humble, honest, and that we are struggling every day to do what is right.

The story of Joash can seem disheartening. If he, with all of his advantages, did not remain faithful to God, is there anyone who grows up in the church who will remain faithful? There are not many biblical examples of people who started out serving God and lived their whole lives without ever rebelling against his commands. But there are a few. Joseph, Daniel, and Timothy come to mind as men who apparently served God all their lives and remained faithful. Elijah walked with God all of his life, and then did not have to face death but was taken up into Heaven in a fiery chariot. Those men were certainly not without sin, because the Bible reminds us we have all sinned. But they were men who held on to their integrity, who never had a change of heart about God or turned from him. They assure us that those who grow up knowing God can indeed remain faithful to him.

We should praise God that many cradle Christians continue to serve God faithfully throughout life. We are all sinners, but we do not all have to go through the pain of a prodigal-son experience. Some learn to throw themselves on the mercy of God early in their childhood, and they continue to depend on his grace throughout life. Those people have a special calling from God. Jesus said, "From everyone who has been given much, much will be demanded" (Luke 12:48). Parents should strive to instill that kind of faithfulness in their children—the kind of faithfulness that Daniel, Joseph, Timothy, and others expressed. That is the kind of faithfulness that will last for eternity.

> Let us not become weary in doing good, for at the proper time, we will reap a harvest if we do not give up (Galatians 6:9).

---

[1]From David Barton, video lecture, *America's Godly Heritage*, (Aledo, TX: Wallbuilders, 1990, 1992).

[2]David Faust, *Growing Churches, Growing Leaders: How to Lead a Growing Church and Live a Balanced Life* (Joplin: College Press, 1994), p. 147.

[3]Faust, *Growing Churches*, p. 148.

[4]Faust, *Growing Churches*, p. 148.

[5]Faust, *Growing Churches*, p. 149.

CHAPTER TEN

Nurture Giftedness

Jesus

Luke 1:26-38; 2:1-20

Jesus was no ordinary child. Perhaps that explains why Christmas is no ordinary day. A novel Christmas card reads, "Christmas is just plain weird. What other time of the year do you sit in front of a dead tree in your living room and eat candy out of your socks?"

Jesus' birthday doesn't compare with the birthday of any other famous person. Years ago, the post offices would be closed on February 22 to celebrate the birthday of George Washington, the father of our country. But the rest of us would hardly notice until our mail wasn't delivered. At the mall, special songs about George Washington are not played on the intercom system during the month of his birthday. School is not even dismissed and cards are not exchanged. People don't greet each other by saying, "Merry Washington's Birthday!"

We don't bring a tree into the house or hang socks on the mantle to remember presidents of the United States or other famous people. You probably cannot recall how you celebrated Abraham Lincoln's birthday last year, or what gifts were exchanged. Do you remember how you celebrated the Wright brothers' birthdays, or Martin Luther King's birthday, or Thomas Edison's or the apostle Paul's?

Almost anyone can tell you on which day of the year we celebrate the birth of Jesus. It is true that Christmas is often too commercialized, and it is true that Jesus was probably not born exactly on December 25. But whether you are a believer or a skeptic, you must admit that no other birthday compares to Jesus'. The pageants, Christmas carols, nativity scenes, decorations, gift exchanges, family gatherings, and church services are incomparable to any other celebration throughout the year.

The Bible predicted that God would give him a name that would be above every name (Philippians 2:9), which has certainly come true. The atheist must be galled by all of the attention given to Jesus during Christmastime. But the celebration of Jesus' birthday should be special because Jesus was unlike any other child. He was God in the flesh, coming to be the Savior of the world.

What a responsibility for Mary and Joseph! Caring for a normal child can be intimidating enough. But Mary and Joseph were entrusted with the one who was "destined to cause the falling and rising of many in Israel" (Luke 2:34). On that first Christmas night they must have felt overwhelmed with the responsibility of nurturing the Messiah.

Though no other child before or since has been born with the giftedness of Jesus, because he was God in the flesh, the Bible does indicate that all of us are gifted (Romans 12:6). It is the responsibility of parents to nurture that giftedness. "Train a child in the way he should go," the Bible tells us, "and when he is old he will not turn from it" (Proverbs 22:6).

In this chapter, we will study Jesus' giftedness as it was predicted, confirmed, and demonstrated to Mary and Joseph. Though Jesus was perfect, his earthly parents were not. Like all parents, Mary and Joseph did some things very well and also made some mistakes. From them we can learn how to nurture the giftedness in our own children.

His Giftedness Predicted

In the sixth month, God sent the angel Gabriel to Nazareth, a town in Galilee, to a virgin pledged to be married to a man named Joseph, a descendant of David. The virgin's name was Mary. The angel went to her and said, "Greetings, you who are highly favored! The Lord is with you."

Mary was greatly troubled at his words and wondered what kind of greeting this might be (Luke 1:26-29).

We are so familiar with the story of Jesus' birth that it sometimes loses its impact. What a frightening experience it must have been for Mary! Picture being in a room where you think you are completely alone. Suddenly, out of nowhere someone appears. And not just anyone, but an extraterrestrial being! You jump, your heart pounds, and you brace yourself for "fight or flight." Mary was terrified.

"But the angel said to her, 'Do not be afraid, Mary, you have found favor with God'" (Luke 1:30). Angels do not always come bearing good news. An angel came to Lot to tell him his city was going to be destroyed and he must get out. Later, an angel would tell Joseph he must get up and flee to Egypt because Herod wanted to kill the baby Jesus.

But this angel had good news.

> You will be with child and give birth to a son, and you are to give him the name Jesus. He will be great and will be called the Son of the Most High. The Lord God will give him the throne of his father David, and he will reign over the house of Jacob forever; his kingdom will never end (Luke 1:31-33).

Mary was not only terrified by the angel's appearance, she was also troubled by his announcement. "'How will this be,' Mary asked the angel, 'since I am a virgin?'" (Luke 1:34).

Mary had seen the consequences older girls were forced to suffer if they got pregnant out of wedlock. She had promised herself that it would never happen to her. She loved her fiancé Joseph, but she had never slept with him. She knew that true love waits.

Because of her purity, she was dumbfounded. "How can this be?" she thought. "How could I be pregnant?" The first to question the virgin birth was Mary herself.

> The angel answered, "The Holy Spirit will come upon you, and the power of the Most High will overshadow you. So the holy one to be born will be called the Son of God" (Luke 1:35).

People have been skeptical and have ridiculed the doctrine of the virgin birth for years. But is the creature greater than the creator? Scientists are now able to practice in vitro fertilization: implanting the seed of the man into the womb of a woman.

What a breakthrough in genetics! But that is nothing new to God. About 2,000 years ago he implanted his own seed into a righteous young woman named Mary. Through the power of the Holy Spirit she conceived and gave birth to the Son of God.

The angel said, "Nothing is impossible with God" (Luke 1:37).

Mary responded: "I am the Lord's servant, and I am willing to do whatever he wants. May everything you said come true" (Luke 1:38, *The Living Bible* paraphrase).

Mary was elated that God had selected her, but she also recognized the awesome responsibility that she had been given to rear such an exceptional child.

His Giftedness Confirmed

Mary and Joseph traveled to Bethlehem to register for a special tax.

> While they were there, the time came for the baby to be born, and she gave birth to her firstborn, a son. She wrapped him in cloths and placed him in a manger, because there was no room for them in the inn (Luke 2:6, 7).

Mary must have been disappointed. She had certainly imagined that the birth of the Messiah would be dramatic. People would be celebrating, relatives embracing, parents glowing, everyone affirming the giftedness of this special child. Instead, she was lying in a barn, miles from home, where no one but Joseph even knew the baby had been born.

Several hours after we brought our first child home from the hospital, I discovered my wife lying in bed crying. She does not cry very often, so I wondered what could possibly be wrong. She told me there was really nothing wrong; she was just a little down. I soon learned that it is common for new mothers to experience a little depression, a letdown, following the excitement of the birth.

I wonder if Mary experienced some feelings of sadness. Her child was no ordinary child. He was the Son of God, destined to take over the throne of David. She must have wondered why the spotlight wasn't on the stable. Why weren't others excited? Why did she have no help? Why did he have to be born in a barn? Where was God?

But God in his wisdom confirmed the greatness of his child through several people.

The Shepherds

When there was a knock on the barn door that night, Mary and Joseph must have thought a group of local dignitaries had come to welcome the Christ child. Instead, they were greeted by some rough and uneducated sheepherders. Shepherds did not have a good reputation in those days. In fact, they were so known for exaggeration and lying that in some cases their testimony was not even admissible in court! They were the brunt of many jokes and were unwelcome at most social events. Most people held shepherds in contempt.

So here were these dirty, smelly shepherds appearing to see the Christ child. These were not the kind of people you want touching and kissing your newborn baby—but Mary and Joseph probably welcomed them. They were glad to have others share in their excitement, and the shepherds were probably the only ones who came to the stable that night.

The shepherds revealed a remarkable story. They insisted that an angel had appeared to them and had told them to come see this baby in a manger, who was the Savior, Christ the Lord. Luke tells us that Mary "treasured up all these things and pondered them in her heart" (Luke 2:19). A mother today might keep a baby book where she saves a lock of the baby's hair, a hand print, a spoon, and many pictures. Mary didn't have a baby book or photographs, but she would never forget the incredible story the shepherds told or their appreciation for the greatness of her child.

Simeon and Anna

When Jesus was about six weeks old, Joseph and Mary took him to the temple. Two elderly people met them there and began doting over the baby.

Having strangers dote over a baby is nothing abnormal. Parents usually love it when people notice their baby. "That's the cutest baby!" they'll say. "Come see this baby! This child is adorable! You should have that child in movies!" I've seen complete strangers ask to hold someone's newborn baby. But these two strangers did not dote over Jesus the way most strangers do.

The Bible says the Holy Spirit led Simeon, a godly old man, to come to the temple to see Jesus. God had revealed to Simon that he would not die until he had seen the Messiah. When Mary and Joseph brought the child into the temple,

> Simeon took him in his arms and praised God, saying: "Sovereign Lord, as you have promised, you now dismiss your servant in peace. For my eyes have seen your salvation, which you have prepared in the sight of all people . . ." (Luke 2:28-31).

Just then an eighty-four-year-old prophetess named Anna came and gave a similar confirmation.

> Coming up to them at that very moment, she gave thanks to God and spoke about the child to all who were looking forward to the redemption of Jerusalem (Luke 2:38).

Joseph and Mary must have been both proud and amazed. Luke writes that they "marveled" at what was said about Jesus (Luke 2:33).

The Wise Men

Some mysterious men from the east also came to pay tribute to Jesus.

> After Jesus was born in Bethlehem in Judea, during the time of King Herod, Magi from the east came to Jerusalem and asked, "Where is the one who has been born king of the Jews? We saw his star in the east and have come to worship him" (Matthew 2:1, 2).

If I were ever asked to direct a Christmas pageant (the chances are slim), I would make a change from the traditional nativity scene. I would like to see the wise men visiting Jesus in a separate scene, not at the stable, but in a house. Read carefully:

> The star they had seen in the east went ahead of them until it stopped over the place where the child was. When they saw the star, they were overjoyed. On coming to the *house*, they saw the child with his mother Mary, and they bowed down and worshiped him (Matthew 2:9-11, emphasis added).

By the time the wise men reached them, Joseph and Mary were staying in a house in Bethlehem. Maybe the innkeeper took them to his home or someone else provided hospitality. Or they may even have had their own home in Bethlehem by this time. But I doubt you will ever see a Christmas pageant where the wise men visit Jesus in someone's house. It not only would require a scene change and a lot more work, but everyone in the audience would think the director messed up the story!

God confirmed the specialness of his Son through a variety of people. The shepherds, Simeon and Anna, and the wise men had all worshiped the Christ child. Rich and poor, Jew and Gentile, male and female, old and young—they all came to honor this child. The Lord was confirming that Jesus had come into the world to be the Savior of all people.

His Giftedness Demonstrated

It wasn't long before Jesus himself began to demonstrate his giftedness.

Jesus as a Child

We have no idea what kind of infancy Jesus had, except for one instance that Matthew records. Shortly after the visit of the wise men, Joseph and Mary fled with Jesus to Egypt. Joseph had been warned in a dream that King Herod, in a jealous fury, was going to try to kill Jesus. Joseph and Mary learned early that if a child is exceptional in any way, he is vulnerable to attack.

Jealous people will say hateful things and seek to undermine a child's potential. That is the reason extraordinary children need extraordinary parents who will patiently encourage them when others reject or ridicule them.

After two years, they returned to Nazareth. Luke summarizes the first twelve years of Jesus' life in one verse: "And the child grew and became strong; he was filled with wisdom, and the grace of God was upon him" (Luke 2:40).

Even when Jesus was still a child, it was obvious to Mary and others that he had a special sensitivity to spiritual things.

Jesus as an Adolescent

When Jesus was twelve years old, his parents took him to worship in Jerusalem as they did every year. When they headed back to Nazareth, Joseph thought Jesus was with his mother. Mary thought he was with Joseph. The men would usually stay behind to break up camp and then catch up with the women later in the evening. When they met that night, they discovered that Jesus was not with either of them.

They must have been terrified. They rushed back to Jerusalem, assuming he had lost his way in the city among the thousands of tourists who had gathered there.

Years ago, when our boys were twelve and eight, we were vacationing in California and took a tour of the Queen Mary, one of the world's largest ships. Phil, the younger of the two boys, wandered off and we couldn't find him. For about ten minutes we were a little frightened. To be that far away from home and be separated from one of your young children is disturbing. At the time, I wasn't afraid that someone was going to kidnap a child like Phil, but I was concerned that he would soon be frightened. In reality, when we finally found him, he wasn't the least concerned.

Mary and Joseph were in a panic. They had already been separated from Jesus for twelve hours, and they had to wonder how they would ever find him. They retraced their steps back to Jerusalem and then back to the temple, expecting that if they did find Jesus he would be petrified. It took them *three days* to find him!

> After three days they found him in the temple courts, sitting among the teachers, listening to them and asking questions. Everyone who heard him was amazed at his understanding and his answers (Luke 2:46, 47).

When Jesus was the age of a sixth-grader, it was obvious to others that he was no ordinary child. His keen mind and his ability to understand spiritual truths delighted even the rabbis.

> When his parents saw him they were astonished. His mother said to him, "Son, why have you treated us like this? Your father and I have been anxiously searching for you" (Luke 2:48).

Mary had imagined that Jesus would be petrified if she ever found him. Instead, he was enjoying himself in the classroom.

Perhaps Mary was disturbed that he was getting along so well without her.

"Why were you searching for me," he asked. "Didn't you know I had to be in my Father's house?" (Luke 2:49).

Jesus was not being rebellious as some adolescents can be. I saw a sign in a restaurant that read,

Children, tired of being harassed by your stupid parents? Act now! Move out, get a job, and pay your own bills while you still know everything!

But Jesus was not being flippant. He knew, even at such a young age, who his heavenly Father was. He was telling the truth.

But they did not understand what he was saying to them.
Then he went down to Nazareth with them and was obedient to them. But his mother treasured all these things in her heart (Luke 2:50, 51).

Mary continued keeping a mental scrapbook, pondering in her heart the special events and the comments about her son that proved to her he was a gifted child.

Luke then bridges an eighteen-year gap of history, from the time Jesus was twelve until he was thirty, with one verse: "And Jesus grew in wisdom and stature, and in favor with God and man" (Luke 2:52).

Jesus as an Adult

John 2 records another interaction between Jesus and Mary, this time when Jesus was thirty years old. Jesus and his family were attending a wedding reception in Cana when the host ran out of wine.

Weddings are tense times. I have seen some strange things happen at weddings. I have seen people faint; I have seen them cry; I've even seen people giggle uncontrollably. I've heard fathers, when asked who gives the woman to be married, respond by saying, "My mother and I"! I've seen fathers trip on the bride's dress and fall into the front pew.

I once told a groom he could kiss the bride, and instead of lifting the veil back from her face and placing it behind her head, he pulled it toward himself, ducked up underneath it, kissed her, and then put it back down!

Tim Coop, a friend of mine, was performing a wedding ceremony when the bride began giggling nervously. He was in the middle of the vows and had asked her to repeat, "Till death do us part." She kept giggling and couldn't get it out. He waited until she regained her composure and said, "Till death do us part." She giggled again. When she stopped, he tried once more: "Till death do us part." Again, the giggling started. Finally he said, "Well, would you settle for a couple of years?"

Ministers sometimes get nervous, too. I've asked the groom to "put the ring on the third hand of her left finger."

Weddings can be tense and produce awkward moments. When the host ran out of wine at the wedding reception in Cana, it was a stressful and potentially embarrassing situation. The host was probably a relative of Mary's and was at his wits' end. Mary must have said, "Don't worry, my son Jesus is here. He always knows what to do."

> When the wine was gone, Jesus' mother said to him, "They have no more wine."
>
> "Dear woman, why do you involve me?" Jesus asked. "My time has not yet come."
>
> His mother said to the servants, "Do whatever he tells you" (John 2:3-5).

Mary refused to take no for an answer, and gently nudged her son into action. Though he had never before performed a miracle, she knew his giftedness, and she was confident he could do something to help.

Jesus told the servants to fill the nearby jars with water and then take them to the man in charge of the banquet. When they did as Jesus had instructed, they discovered that the water had been transformed into wine.

When a little boy was asked by his father what they had learned in Sunday school, he told him the story of Jesus' turning water into wine. "What does that teach you?" the father asked.

The boy said, "Whenever you have a wedding, you'd better invite Jesus."

Jesus' first miracle was performed at the prompting of his mother, who had believed in and nurtured his giftedness.

This, the first of his miraculous signs, Jesus performed at Cana in Galilee. He thus revealed his glory, and his disciples put their faith in him (John 2:11).

Lessons to Be Learned

None of us will ever nurture a Messiah, but every child has distinctive and unique gifts that can be used by God.

Identify and Encourage Giftedness in Your Child

Remember, each child is unique—one of a kind.

Boys and girls can be compliant or headstrong, easygoing or a handful. They can be artistic or math-minded, competitive or casual, sloppy or compulsive cleaners. A parent's responsibility is to round off the edges of the less-desired traits and encourage the development of good attributes. It's important for children's self-esteem that they excel at *something*.[1]

Our senior citizens minister, John Faust, was an excellent athlete as a young man. But neither of his sons took an interest in sports. His son Rob is a musician, and his son Rich is an artist. John says he often watched Super Bowls and basketball games alone, but he never chastised or ridiculed his sons for not sharing his interests, though it was sometimes difficult for him to keep quiet. However, he spoke of a gratifying experience he recently had on Thanksgiving Day. The entire Faust clan was present and they were sharing things they were thankful for. John's son Rich, who is in college studying art, said, "I'm thankful for my mother and dad who have been a big help to me." I've known other parents who have pushed their children in the wrong direction, and the results are just the opposite.

Even Gifted Children Should Learn Obedience

Jesus was a special child, yet we read that he was still obeying his parents when he was an adolescent (Luke 2:51).

Parents and other adults have a tendency to relax discipline if the child is gifted. A child may get special treatment because he is a great athlete. Another may practically get away with murder because she is cute or another because he has a great sense of humor. We might also be tempted to let a child get by with disobedience if he has a handicap, because we feel sorry for him.

But gifted children—sometimes even more so than an average child—need to learn submission. Other people are going to give them favors, and they will be tempted to get by on their talent or charm alone. If they are ever to learn to have a submissive heart toward God, they will need some adults in their lives who do not make concessions because of their giftedness.

There was a recent article in our local paper titled, "A Leg Up On Life." It was about Bonnie Consolo, a woman who was born without arms. She said she does not like to be called "disabled," and she has proven why. She uses her feet to drive a car, operate a computer, sign checks, grocery shop, and feed and clothe herself.

She said that when she was growing up, her parents treated her just like they treated her brothers and sisters. That must have been difficult for the parents to do. It would be tempting to look at a toddler with no arms and want to pity her, pamper her, and do everything for her. But Bonnie's parents had the wisdom to prepare her for life by allowing her to learn independence and by disciplining her like a normal child, though that must have taken an incredible amount of patience and tough love.[2]

Release the Child When It Is Time

The time for releasing a child probably comes earlier than expected when the child is gifted. It was difficult for Mary to see Jesus doing well without her when he was only twelve years old, but he was beginning to wean himself away from her. Some of the most painful moments for parents come when we realize that our children are moving away from us. Those moments begin with the first day of school and continue through their first date, the first day of college, getting married, and moving out of town. But a wise parent knows when to hold on and when to let go. A child's giftedness cannot be developed fully without freedom.

Dave Kennedy was the minister of the South Jefferson Christian Church in Louisville for several years. He then accepted a new ministry in Danville, Illinois, just prior to his older daughter Lisa's senior year of high school. She was heartbroken. She finally came to him and said, "Dad, I don't want to move. I would like to stay here in Louisville with a family in the church and finish my senior year here."

Dave told her that she was not allowed to stay, but must move with the family.

Dave is close to Lisa, and he says they hardly ever exchange harsh words. But she cried and pouted, and he shouted and pouted for several days. Finally, he went into her room one night and sat on the edge of her bed. "Do you really want to stay here?" he asked.

"Dad," she said, "I really do. Remember, Dad, in one of your sermons you said, 'When you love something, let it go; if it comes back to you it's yours, but if it doesn't, it never was yours'?"

Dave says, "I hate it when they do that! Why couldn't she remember me saying, 'Honor your father and mother'? Now I say, 'If you love something and it won't come back, hunt it down and shoot it!'"

Dave sensed that Lisa was mature enough to handle staying in Louisville, and he was wise enough to give her the freedom she needed. Lisa was permitted to stay. She had a fine senior year and turned out to be a wonderful Christian lady. In fact, a few years later, she began working on the church staff with her father as the director of the day-care.

That decision would not have been right in every situation. Circumstances, maturity, and temperament vary. But parents need to pray for the wisdom to recognize the proper time to release their children into the world.

Jesus was a special child. Mary sensed it when the angels announced the virgin birth. It was confirmed to her by Anna, Simeon, the shepherds, and the wise men. And it was demonstrated in the life of Jesus through his powerful preaching, extraordinary teaching, and miraculous healings.

A popular contemporary Christian song, "Mary, Did You Know?" asks Mary whether she realized when Jesus was born that he would do the many special things he would do. One of the questions it asks is, "Mary, did you know that this child you delivered would one day deliver you?" She knew he was special. She knew he was God's Son. The angel had told her

133

that. But there was no way Mary could have known or understood just *how* special Jesus was. She expected him to rule from a throne—that was the popular understanding of the role of the Messiah. When he was crucified, Mary was brokenhearted and confused. As Simeon had prophesied, a sword had pierced her soul (Luke 2:35).

But when Jesus was raised from the dead, she understood and rejoiced. Jesus had died for the sins of the world, and that included her own sins.

None of us will be asked, as Mary was, to rear the Messiah. But the Bible says that we all have different gifts according to the grace God has given us (Romans 12:6). We need to recognize those gifts in our children. We need to encourage our kids to become all that God has intended them to be. We must demand that they be submissive to authority so they can learn to be submissive to God's authority. Then, at the proper time, we must release them so they can freely exercise those gifts to the glory of God.

---

[1]Greg Johnson and Mike Yorkey, *Faithful Parents, Faithful Kids* (Wheaton: Tyndale, 1993), p. 60.

[2]Louisville *Courier Journal,* November 22, 1993

CHAPTER ELEVEN

Saturate With Scripture

Timothy

2 Timothy 1, 3; Deuteronomy 6

T he following ironic message was found on an airplane's emergency instructions card: "If you can't read this, please notify a stewardess."

American educators are concerned because more and more Americans are growing up illiterate. Some high school graduates can barely read their diplomas. Christians should be concerned about this issue as well. Throughout history, especially in America, Christians have led the charge to educate the populace for one main reason: so that people will be able to read the Bible.

Our problem today is then twofold. Not only should we be concerned that many people cannot read at all, but both those who can read and those who cannot read do not know the Scriptures. For more than 200 years in America, the education system helped the church teach young people the Bible. Now, education and the church are at odds over the Bible. As a result, biblical illiteracy is at an all-time high.

I heard of a preacher who went to the fourth-grade boys Sunday school class and asked, "Who caused the walls of Jericho to fall down?"

One little guy said, "It wasn't me, preacher."

The preacher looked at the Sunday school teacher and said, "Can you believe that?"

The teacher said, "Preacher, I've known the boy a long time and he's always been honest. I'm sure it wasn't him."

The preacher was so upset over their biblical ignorance that he called an elders' meeting and told them what had happened.

One of the elders spoke up and said, "Let's not argue over who did what. Let's just pay for the damages to the wall and forget it ever happened."

That story always gets a laugh, but it is really no laughing matter. There is a dire need for young and old alike to know and follow the Word of God. We know that teen pregnancy, violent crime, and divorce have all shot up in America since 1963, when the Bible was taken out of the schools. There seems to be a definite connection between an ignorance of God's Word and a decadent society.

However, Christians should not blame the educational system. According to the Bible, the ultimate responsibility for teaching the Word of God is given to Christian parents. If you want to inoculate your children against the evils and temptations they will face in the world, fill their minds with the Word of God. If you want to improve the culture for the next generation, saturate your children with Scripture.

While the primary responsibility for teaching the Bible to children is the parents', we are all accountable to God for what we teach and demonstrate to children (Matthew 18:6). Every adult Christian should care enough about the next generation to take part in teaching and applying the Scriptures to young people. Some will do it in the role of teacher, presenting lessons they have prepared for the children. More of us will simply do it in life, modeling attitudes and behaviors that are either consistent or inconsistent with God's Word. Either way, we teach some powerful lessons.

Timothy was Paul's dear friend and apprentice. The last thing Paul wrote, as far as we know, was his second letter to Timothy. Tucked away in this letter is a verse that gives us insight into why Timothy became such an influential leader in the early church. The lessons learned from this verse should motivate us to saturate our children with the Scriptures.

I have been reminded of your sincere faith, which first lived in your grandmother Lois and in your mother Eunice and, I am persuaded, now lives in you also (2 Timothy 1:5).

The Challenges Eunice Faced

It must have been difficult for Eunice to rear a godly child. It is never easy, but it would have been especially challenging in Eunice's case for several reasons.

First, Timothy was being reared in a pagan Roman environment. Worldly temptations were constantly inviting him to stray from moral values. Greek and Roman belief in many gods continually challenged his faith in the one true and living God. Most of his peers would have held pagan beliefs, tempting Timothy to compromise in order to fit in.

Second, some Bible students think Timothy may not have been a strong-willed person by nature. From what Paul tells him in such passages as 1 Timothy 4:12-14 and 2 Timothy 1:6-8, they conclude Timothy was tempted to be too timid and passive at times. Some people find it difficult to be assertive. It requires a conscious and continual effort on their part to stand up for what they believe.

Third, Timothy's father was a Gentile and possibly a non-believer (Acts 16:1). Some theologians speculate that Timothy's father may have died when Timothy was in his early teens. That certainly would have been an added burden to both Timothy and his mother, and would have increased the odds that Timothy would succumb to the pressures of the world.

But somehow, Timothy's mother had beaten the odds. The seed of God's truth that she had planted in Timothy produced a harvest of faith.

The Word Eunice Taught

To my knowledge, Timothy is the only New Testament example of a second-generation Christian. Since the church had just begun, most Christians had been converted as adults. But Timothy's mother and grandmother had influenced him for Christ when he was still a young man. He may have been the first second-generation Christian to take a leadership position in the New Testament church.

We are rightfully thrilled when we hear dramatic "prodigal son" stories, testimonies from people who have lived a worldly life and then have come to know Christ. But, as noted earlier, sometimes we are tempted to feel less spiritual if our conversion wasn't so dramatic. Perhaps Timothy was tempted to feel that way. He had known Christ since he was a young boy. He had no dramatic conversion story like his hero, the apostle Paul.

My mother reared six children who today are all committed Christians and have raised Christian families of their own. None of us has a dramatic conversion story. Instead, we all have wonderful memories of growing up in a godly home. Someone asked my mother what her formula was for rearing children in the Lord. She said, "I would fill them with the Word and then pray like mad."

Though Timothy did not have a dramatic conversion story, God used him in dramatic ways to lead others to Christ. The Word of God has the power not only to change lives, but to keep people in a right relationship with the Father. Notice another passage from Paul to Timothy, where Paul gives credit for Timothy's faith to those who took the time to teach him the Holy Scriptures:

> But as for you, continue in what you have learned and have become convinced of, because you know *those from whom you have learned it*, and how *from infancy* you have known the holy Scriptures, which are able to make you wise for salvation through faith in Christ Jesus (2 Timothy 3:14, 15, emphasis added).

The Help Eunice Received

Let's recognize two important people who helped strengthen Timothy's faith besides his mother Eunice. Again we are reminded of the influence that we have over children, even when they are not our own.

Paul mentioned not only Timothy's mother Eunice but also his grandmother, Lois. How do you suppose Lois taught the Word to Timothy? Can you see her teaching Timothy Scripture songs, telling him bedtime stories about the great heroes of the faith, taking him to the synagogue, teaching him to pray, reminding him of the great heritage from which he had come?

God blessed Timothy with a godly grandmother who had the time to spend with him to saturate him with the holy Scriptures.

But we cannot minimize the influence that the great apostle Paul had in the life of Timothy. Paul took Timothy under his wing when Timothy was still a young man, and Timothy spent fifteen years as Paul's understudy. It is impossible to know what might have happened to Timothy if Paul had never entered the picture. He may never have received the influence of a positive male role model. Perhaps when he reached adulthood, he would have foolishly dismissed all the things he had been taught as things only women are supposed to think about. But Timothy saw those truths he had been taught from infancy lived out in a man he admired and respected. Then he followed Paul's example and became a great leader in the early church.

There are a lot of young people growing up today who have no father living at home, and many others who have never seen a man live a godly life. As they grow up, they will be vulnerable. They need Christian men full of integrity to adopt them spiritually, to be their companions, to encourage them and be positive role models.

Bobby Knight was interviewed by David Letterman on his *Late Show*. As I recall, Knight made the statement, "Kids haven't changed over the years, but adults have."

Letterman said, "But adults were at one time kids, Bobby."

"Yeah," Knight said, "But they had better adults than the kids have today."

Knight should know.

A few years ago, Bonnie Tyler sang, "I Need a Hero." When we look to the world, we don't see very many heroes. We see their reputations become tarnished. It surfaces that our hero has a gambling habit; another has been sexually immoral; another has been accused of molesting children; still another is accused of murdering his wife. Through time, we discover that our man-made heroes are far from perfect. They have feet of clay.

Without some standards to go by, many children accept their heroes' faults as valid role models. They imitate the bad as well as the good. Since they like the athlete or the rock star, they accept that person's behavior as proper. Whether they want to or not, famous people become role models, and too many of them are inferior heroes.

Children need some heroes like the ones Timothy found in his grandmother Lois, his mother Eunice, and his friend and mentor, the apostle Paul.

Why Should We Teach the Bible to Our Children?

Paul told Timothy the Scriptures that had so dramatically influenced Timothy's life were "God-breathed":

> All Scripture is God-breathed and is useful for teaching, rebuking, correcting and training in righteousness, so that the man of God may be thoroughly equipped for every good work (2 Timothy 3:16, 17).

When God formed man from the dust of the ground, he breathed into his nostrils the breath of life, and man became a living soul (Genesis 2:7). When men of God began writing down the words of the Bible, God breathed into it as well, so that the Bible would come to life.

> For the Word of God is living and active. Sharper than any double-edged sword, it penetrates even to dividing soul and spirit, joints and marrow; it judges the thoughts and attitudes of the heart (Hebrews 4:12).

In addition to the fact that the Bible is alive, true, and is the inspired Word of God, let's consider several other reasons why we should spend time teaching our children the Word of God:

The Bible Teaches Children the Will of God

There is no other way for a child to know for sure what God wants. Only the Bible gives definite guidelines and absolute truths to live by. Only in the Bible can we discover what direction God wants us to take in life.

> Your word is a lamp to my feet and a light for my path (Psalm 119:105).

The Bible Is Powerful

It has the power to transform lives, to save souls, to instill us with confidence. One author said, "Some books are for our information; some for our inspiration; the Bible is for our transformation."

> I am not ashamed of the gospel, because it is the power of God for the salvation of everyone who believes (Romans 1:16).

The Bible Fortifies Against Sin

The Bible not only tells us what is right and wrong, it also inspires us to do what is right.

> Blessed is the man who does not walk in the counsel of the wicked or stand in the way of sinners or sit in the seat of mockers. But his delight is in the law of the LORD, and on his law he meditates day and night (Psalm 1:1, 2).

> I have hidden your word in my heart that I might not sin against you (Psalm 119:11).

God's Word Feeds the Soul

As young people today chase after things they think will satisfy them, we need to lead them to something that can truly feed their souls.

> How sweet are your words to my taste, sweeter than honey to my mouth! (Psalm 119:103).

> When your words came, I ate them; they were my joy and my heart's delight, for I bear your name, O LORD God Almighty (Jeremiah 15:16).

When Should We Teach the Bible to Our Children?

Occasionally someone will say, "I don't want to force my religion on my children. That will have to be their own choice." The folly of such a statement is obvious. We make our children go to school, we make them take medicine, we make them go to bed on time, we make them brush their teeth and do other things that are good for them. Why should we not demand that they learn the Bible? If the Word of God is true, and if their lives truly would be better with God's Word hidden in their hearts, it makes sense for parents to teach their children whenever and wherever possible the truths that are in the Scriptures.

Let's return to a Scripture we've noted before:

> Love the Lord your God with all your heart and with all your soul and with all your strength. These commandments that I give you

today are to be upon your hearts. Impress them on your children. Talk about them when you sit at home and when you walk along the road, when you lie down and when you get up. Tie them as symbols on your hands and bind them on your foreheads. Write them on the doorframes of your houses and on your gates (Deuteronomy 6:5-9).

That passage gives some practical suggestions as to when you should teach your children the Bible. Teach them "when you sit at home"—perhaps before or after meals. Discuss the Bible "when you walk along the road"—on trips in the car or during walks around the neighborhood. Read Scripture "when you lie down"—before bed—"and when you get up"—in the morning.

I've mentioned before that when our boys were home, our family would have devotions every night before we went to bed. When they were younger, we read a Bible-story book that was written for children. Every page would be a one- or two-paragraph summary of a famous Bible story, and then there would be some questions to answer at the end. My sons say they can still remember the pictures from their first Bible-story book.

Our associate minister, Dave Stone, speaks of similar experiences when he was growing up. His mother would quiz them every night on a particular passage of Scripture that they were studying. She recorded in a notebook the questions she asked and how many of them each boy was able to answer correctly. Dave said his mother recently found one of those old notebooks and sent it to him. He said he thinks he knew the Bible better at age five than he does today! He asked his mother what kind of reward they received for getting questions right. She said, "I didn't have to give you a reward. You were just so excited to answer questions from the Bible correctly, that was all the reward you needed." If we are creative, we can make learning the Bible an enjoyable activity for our children.

Most of us are creatures of habit, and it would be best if we had a regular time every day when we read the Bible together as a family. However, daily devotions are not commanded in Scripture and should not become a legalistic drudgery. We have to be creative.

V. Gilbert Beers, the president of Scripture Press, has a good perspective:

> I believe our children love the Word of God today because we made our occasional visits into the Bible times of delight. We tried lots of approaches. Sometimes they worked; sometimes they bombed. When they bombed, we admitted it and waited for a better time. Devotions at our house became irregularly regular times of delight rather than oppressively regular times of drudgery.

Not only would it be wise for us to develop a habit of daily Bible reading as a family, but we should also use everyday opportunities to teach our children about the Lord. The passage in Deuteronomy said we should teach them, "When you walk along the road. . . ."

A two-year-old and her mother were walking one day when the mother said, "Look at those clouds! Didn't God do a good job making those pretty clouds?"

The little girl stopped in her tracks, looked into the sky, gave the thumbs up sign, and said, "Good job, God!"

When we take the time to teach our children about God when they are young, believing in God becomes as natural as any other part of life.

Allen Hadidian said,

> Devotional living is using our everyday experiences and activities to teach our children spiritual truths. It is talking freely with our children about God and making him a part of our everyday conversations. Just as Jesus used common objects such as seeds and soil, pearls and hidden treasures to teach valuable lessons, we can use common objects and experiences as well to help our children see how God is intertwined in every aspect of our lives. This way the simplest activities become opportunities to teach children about God, his Word, his ways and his Son.

How Should We Teach the Bible to Our Children?

The most important way to teach the Bible is by example. We have to demonstrate that what it says is believable and practical. We may take every opportunity to saturate our children with Scripture, but if we come across as less than genuine, we are wasting our time. Our lives must reflect that we, too, believe in the Word we are teaching them.

Gladys Hunt stated it well:

> All of us want the Bible to be a living Book for our children. One truth seems overwhelmingly obvious, however. No matter what technique we use, our own attitude is the key. We must be *genuine*. Our blatant inconsistencies linked with outward piety will battle the authority of the Word of God in our children's lives.[1]

Greg Johnson and Mike Yorkey, the authors of *Faithful Parents, Faithful Kids,* remind us that the chances of raising kids who love and obey God's Word will be greatly increased if they see us opening the Bible more often than Christmas morning when we read Luke 2. Building a hunger for the Bible in our kids begins with our own spiritual appetite. If we don't make much time for God's Word, chances are that our children won't either.

Children are on loan to us from God. He may loan you a group of children for an hour a week, if you teach a Sunday school class. He may loan you a child for one week out of the year when your own children go on vacation and you keep the grandkids. Perhaps he has loaned you a child that you call your own for a lifetime. But even if we call them our own, we must remember that they belong to God. Therefore, we would be wise to take every opportunity to saturate them with his Word.

Dr. James Dobson writes of the first time he realized that his children were on loan from God and needed to be a priority in his life:

> It occurred first in 1969. I was running at an incredible speed, working myself to death like every other man I knew. I once worked seventeen nights straight without being home in the evening. Our five-year-old daughter would stand in the doorway and cry as I left in the morning, knowing she might not see me until the next sunrise.
>
> Although my activities were bringing me professional advancement and the trappings of financial success, my dad was not impressed. He wrote me a lengthy letter, which was to have a sweeping influence on my life. Here is one paragraph of it:

"Danae [referring to our daughter] is growing up in the wickedest section of a world much farther gone into moral decline than the world into which you were born. I have observed that the greatest delusion is to suppose that our children will be devout Christians simply because their parents have been, or that any of them will enter into the Christian faith in any other way than through their parents' deep travail of prayer and faith. But this prayer demands time, time that cannot be given if it is all signed and conscripted and laid on the altar of career ambition. Failure for you at this point would make mere success in your occupation a very pale and washed-out affair, indeed."

Those words, written without accusation or insult, hit me like the blow from a hammer. My number one responsibility is to evangelize my own children. In the words of my dad, everything else appears "pale and washed out" when compared with that fervent desire. Unless my son and daughter grasp the faith and take it with them around the track, it matters little how fast they run.[2]

We can't teach our children the Word of God unless we are present to model it for them. Gladys Hunt said, "We demonstrate our confidence in the authority of the Word of God by the way we use it in our homes and by our personal obedience to it."

Saturate your children with Scripture, show them how it permeates your own life, and then pray like mad that the Word of God will take root in their hearts and minds.

---

[1]Gladys Hunt, *Honey for a Child's Heart: The Imaginative Use of Books in Family Life* (Grand Rapids: Zondervan, 1989), p. 100.

[2]Adapted from James C. Dobson, *Straight Talk,* revised edition (Dallas: Word, 1991), pp. 75-79.

CHAPTER TWELVE

Instill
Distinctiveness

Paul's Nephew

Acts 23:12-24

Psychologist Ruth W. Berenda conducted an interesting experiment with teenagers to show how a person handles peer pressure. Groups of adolescents were brought into a room for a test. Each group of ten teenagers was instructed to raise their hands when the proctor pointed to the longest line on a chart. One person in the group did not know that the other nine had been instructed ahead of time to vote for a shorter line, which was not even close to being as long. The psychologist wanted to determine how one person would react when completely surrounded by a large number of people who stood against what was obviously true.

The experiment began with nine teenagers intentionally voting for the wrong line. The stooge would typically glance around, frown in confusion and slip his hand up with the group. The instruction was repeated and the next card was raised. Time after time, the self-conscious "yes man" would sit there saying a short line is longer than a long line, simply because he lacked the courage to challenge the group.[1]

The conformity occurred in about seventy-five percent of the cases, and was true of small children as well as high school students.

That study documented what most of us already know. It is hard to be distinctive. For many, popularity takes precedence over integrity. Peer pressure is an awesome reality.

The Bible compares us to sheep, who are quick to follow others. That's not always bad. We should choose role models who are positive examples because it is helpful to imitate positive characteristics in others. And there are times when we are commanded by God to follow our leaders cooperatively. But the fear of being different often leads people—especially young people—to spiritual and moral disaster. The desire to be liked and accepted by their peers is often the greatest factor in determining how teens will think, feel, and behave.

A 1985 *U.S. News and World Report* article on "Morality" related that seventy-eight percent of young people between the ages of eighteen and twenty-nine don't believe that premarital sex is wrong. A recent *USA Today* article reported that fifty-eight percent of high school students drink beer at least once a week. And according to the twenty-fourth annual *Survey of High School High Achievers*, seventy-eight percent of students admit that they regularly cheat on tests.

If Christians are to pass on the baton of faith, we must teach our children how to stand against peer pressure. They need to be taught to make their own choices, based on Scripture and not culture. If our young people are allowed to go along with the majority, they will be lured into a lifestyle that is opposed to God's will. Parents and other adults must be convinced that it is more important for our Christian children to stand for truth than to be popular. We have to teach the next generation how to live distinctive lives.

In Acts 23 there is recorded the story of a young boy who courageously stood for what was right, though he knew it might cost him his life. The apostle Paul was in prison. A group of Jewish leaders had conspired to kill him as he was being taken from the prison to the courtroom. Somehow Paul's nephew, the son of Paul's sister, discovered the plot against Paul's life and went to the prison to tell his uncle Paul. Paul sent him to the commander, who took the young man aside and asked him what information he had to share (Acts 23:19).

He said: "The Jews have agreed to ask you to bring Paul before the Sanhedrin tomorrow on the pretext of wanting more accurate information about him. Don't give in to them, because more than forty of them are waiting in ambush for him. They have taken an oath not to eat or drink until they have killed him. They are ready now, waiting for your consent to their request" (Acts 23:20, 21).

It took remarkable courage for this young man to walk into the Roman prison and save the life of Paul in this way. It is obvious that he cared more about doing what is right than about going along with the crowd. The lessons we learn from his story will inspire us to instill in our children a desire to stand for truth.

The Pressures He Faced

Paul's nephew had to stand for what was right despite the pressures he might have faced to compromise his values.

Fear

Paul's nephew potentially had much to fear. If the Jewish men who were plotting against Paul discovered who had ruined their plot, it is likely they would have gone after this young man.

It also must have been a fearful thing to walk into the Roman jail to find Paul. This was a fortress on the northwest corner of the temple. It was the living quarters for many Roman soldiers, including the commander, as well as a prison. It had to be intimidating for a young Jewish boy to walk into the barracks of the occupying Roman army!

Besides that, what if he were seen? We don't know how he learned of the plot against Paul—but what if the person who revealed the plot to him saw him go into the barracks? Once the plot had failed, it would have been easy to figure out why the boy had gone to the barracks.

Peers

It is very possible that one of his peers revealed to him the plot against Paul's life. Perhaps he was friends with the son of one of the conspirators, and the son did not know his relation to the apostle Paul. It certainly was not the accepted behavior for a young boy to be hanging around with prisoners and Roman soldiers. It would not have been the "cool" thing for Jewish teenagers to do. It is possible that Paul's nephew stood to lose some friends, or at least face some ridicule, for his bold steps.

My eighth-grade gym class included six weeks of formal dancing lessons. I suppose they felt we needed some culture. But my parents disapproved of dancing, and I was sent to school with a note from my parents that I was not permitted to dance because it was against my religion. I had to sit on the stage with a Mennonite boy and watch my friends dance by.

My friends said, "Russell, why aren't you dancing?"

It killed me to have to say, "It's against my religion." They looked at me like I was a kook! I liked my popularity, so for the rest of the period I compromised by making fun of them.

At the next session, there were five guys who had notes from their parents saying it was against their religion to dance! The gym teacher didn't buy it. He made them get back out on the floor and sent me to a study hall.

Nobody likes to be different. But Paul's nephew didn't worry about what his friends might think. He was determined to do what was right.

The Qualities He Exhibited

Paul's nephew demonstrated at least three qualities that we need to cultivate in our young people today.

Decisiveness

This young man did not have trouble making a decision. He did not say, "I think there might be a plot against Paul's life and maybe I should do something about it." He acted. And when he was given a chance to speak to the commander, he told him exactly what was going to happen. "Don't give in to them," he told the commander (Acts 23:21). Giving orders to a Roman commander was a pretty bold act for a young Jewish boy!

Charisma

This young man knew how to give a persuasive speech! The Roman commander listened to his story and acted upon it. Strictly on the advice of Paul's nephew, the commander changed plans and sent a detachment of 470 troops with Paul so that he might safely make it to his destination.

Paul's nephew won over the commander with his words.

Paul once told Timothy, "Don't let anyone look down on you because you are young, but set an example for the believers in speech, in life, in love, in faith and in purity" (1 Timothy 4:12).

It takes some charisma to win over a commander in the Roman army. It is especially impressive when a young person develops charisma and is able to relate to adults the way this young man could.

We need to communicate to our young people that being a Christian doesn't mean being a nerd. There is a difference between being distinctive and being obnoxious. Titus 2:10 says Christians are to behave so that "in every way they will make the teaching about God our Savior attractive."

Sometimes the preaching of the cross is offensive to the world. There are times when our distinctiveness will turn people off. But the Bible says, "If it is possible, as far as it depends on you, live at peace with everyone" (Romans 12:18). We shouldn't deliberately stir up conflict just to be different.

Luke 2:52 reads, "And Jesus grew in wisdom and stature, and in favor with God *and men*" (emphasis added). There ought to be a charisma about us that makes Christianity attractive to others.

Confidence

This young man did not leave any doubt about the truth. He stuck to his story and boldly explained exactly what those in the conspiracy were planning to do.

Our goal should be to instruct our children in such a way that they are confident of their faith. We want them to stand before a class and state their belief in creation without being defensive. We want them to resist sexual advances and unapologetically say they are waiting until marriage. We want them to refuse to accept a friend's copy of an upcoming test because they know unashamedly what is the right thing to do.

Someone said, "A faith that cannot be tested cannot be trusted."

The Success He Experienced

The happy result of this boy's actions demonstrates the reward of being distinctive. Of course, not every encounter when we stand alone for right will end as well. Sometimes we will get hurt—emotionally if not physically. We need to encourage our young people to take a stand even when it is not popular, even when they know they will get burned. The eternal result is always more important than the temporal result. "Our present sufferings are not worth comparing with the glory that will be revealed in us" (Romans 8:18).

At the same time, we need to let our children know that one person can make a difference! They need to know that sometimes even the temporal result is good. Sometimes, it takes just one person to stand up for what is right to create positive changes. That was the case with Paul's nephew.

The Pagan Leaders Became Convinced

In response to what Paul's nephew told him, the commander

> called two of his centurions and ordered them, "Get ready a detachment of two hundred soldiers, seventy horsemen and two hundred spearmen to go to Caesarea at nine tonight. Provide mounts for Paul so that he may be taken safely to Governor Felix" (Acts 23:23, 24).

All of these things were set in motion by one young boy telling the truth. Perhaps these soldiers changed their minds about only a relatively small issue, Paul's journey, in comparison with our eternal journey. But it does show how many lives can be affected if we are simply willing to speak the truth in love.

You can't dispute results. There is one thing that will persuade unbelievers more than anything else: a changed life. People might ignore the Bible, but they cannot deny the power of a transformed life. Loving families, positive attitudes, clean living, and compassionate deeds are irrefutable arguments for our faith.

I met recently with a local education leader who paid our church a great compliment. He said, "Bob, some people in the community take shots at you and Southeast because it is so large. But I want you to know that your best 'P.R.' is the people who go here. The people I encounter are positive about the church and the difference it is making in their lives. No one can refute that."

You will never know what an influence a few positive words of truth have had on another individual.

God Answered the Nephew's Request and Spared Paul's Life

Paul remained a prisoner for close to five years after this, including "two whole years" in Rome (Acts 28:30). From his Roman imprisonment, he wrote four books: Ephesians, Philippians, Colossians, and Philemon. If Paul is the author of Hebrews (as many believe), it is likely he wrote it at about the same time. After his release, he wrote the "pastoral epistles": 1 and 2 Timothy and Titus. None of those books would have been written if his nephew hadn't spoken up clearly and saved his life. Ten years of Paul's ministry followed this boy's courageous act.

The Lesson He Teaches

The events in this story of Paul's nephew should impress upon us the importance of teaching our children that Christians are to be distinctive.

First Peter 2:9 reads, "You are a chosen people [the King James version has "peculiar people" here], a royal priesthood, a holy nation, a people belonging to God, that you may declare the praises of him who called you out of darkness into his wonderful light."

Scott Marmaday, a native American from the Kiowa tribe and professor of literature at USC, related a time when he was a young boy. His father wakened him early one morning and took him to the home of an old squaw. All day long the old squaw sang songs, taught rituals, told stories, and reviewed the history of the Kiowa people. She explained how the Kiowa tribe began. She described buffalo hunts and wars with other tribes. She told of the coming of the white man and of the reservation. That evening as the sun was setting, in the distant hills his father came for him. Marmaday said he had arrived that morning as an average young American boy. But he said, "I left her home a Kiowa."

It is our task to make sure our children leave our homes Christians—ready to stand for the values of our Father.

> For you have heard my vows O God;
> you have given me the heritage of those who fear your name . . .
> Then will I ever sing praise to your name
> and fulfill my vows day after day.
> —Psalm 61: 5, 8

Our children must understand that being a Christian means being distinctive in certain areas.

Moral Values

In December of 1993, *Focus on the Family Magazine* featured an article entitled, "Where are the Cookies?" It told of a mother who is a state health nurse. She has a transparent cookie jar sitting on the dining room buffet filled with condoms. She explained that she has the condoms available for her four children, ages 14 to 21. Since they are not going to abstain from sex anyway, she says, she would rather have them practice safe sex. Two of her kids are sexually active and enjoy choosing their favorite brand in front of their parents. Whenever the jar gets low, the "progressive" mother refills it.

That mother—a professing, church-going Christian—is making several costly mistakes. First, she is allowing her children to believe there is such a thing as "safe sex" outside of God's guidelines for sex. Condoms have nearly a fifteen percent failure rate—and that is only in preventing pregnancy. One has to wonder how much greater the failure rate is in preventing sexually transmitted diseases. Second, she is providing a means for her children to be immoral, and as such is endorsing the behavior. Third, she is relating to them that she expects them to fail to be moral. And she's not baking any chocolate chip cookies!

Senator Daniel Patrick Moynihan said, "We [as a society] are defining deviancy down." He was right. When the attorney general suggests that we legalize drugs, we are defining deviancy down. We are lowering the standards of what our society will deem immoral or unacceptable behavior. As a result, we are losing our society.

For Christians, the standard does not change. We believe that Jesus is the same yesterday, today, and forever. Therefore, as our society continues to define deviancy down, Christians must become increasingly different from the world.

> But among you there must not be even a hint of sexual immorality, or of any kind of impurity . . . because these are improper for God's holy people (Ephesians 5:3).

One of our problems is that we are expecting too little of our children. We begin with the assumption that self-discipline is impossible. But many young people are rebelling against the notion that they are just animals responding to stimuli, that they "are going to do it anyway," so all adults can hope for is to minimize the risk.

Thousands of Christian young people are participating in a program called, "True Love Waits." They are making commitments to be sexually pure until they are married, and they are putting those commitments in written contracts. They are proving that it is indeed possible for them to resist sexual temptation.

World Magazine (December, 1993) ran an article about the "True Love Waits" program. Titled "The Non-Sexual Revolution," the article says, "Christian teenagers are ignoring their elders, and pledging to have no sex before marriage." Melissa Milroy, age sixteen, is quoted as saying, "I know that this is difficult, but what really shocked me was that when the media found out about the program, they were so surprised that there were such things as teenagers who weren't sexually active. It was as if the media never heard of virginity before."

If we can encourage our children to "just say no" to drugs, then we can encourage them to resist premarital sex and alcohol and lying and cheating, too. We simply need to show them there is a better alternative. We must begin long before puberty to train our young people how to be distinctively pure. It begins with other matters before they reach adolescence.

Dress

First Timothy 2:9 says that Christians should dress modestly. *Newsweek* (July 26, 1993) had an article entitled, "That Slut Look in Junior Fashions." The author, Joy Overbeck, told of taking her ten-year-old daughter Meredith shopping. The clothes that Meredith wanted to buy were, according to her mother, clothes that even Cher would have rejected. Meredith accused her mother of not wanting her to grow up. Overbeck wrote, "I don't care anymore if my offspring has a hissy fit in the junior department. She's not wearing the slut look. Let her rant that I'm a hopelessly pathological mom who wants to keep her in pinafores forever. I've shaken the guilt and drawn the line." If parents in the secular world are even beginning to draw the line, why do so many Christian parents lack the courage to do the same?

You can visit the local mall and see ten- and twelve-year-old girls dressed sloppily and suggestively. Grade-school boys are wearing T-shirts with raunchy slogans and pictures of the most pagan rock groups. Those children get compliments and acceptance from their peers because rebellious behavior is a natural inclination of carnal man. The child becomes increasingly dependent on the acceptance of his peers and increasingly resistant to a distinctive life-style.

It is true that styles change, and what is considered immodest in one era can be acceptable in the next. We have gone from the spit curl and "D.A." hairdo, when I was a teen, to earrings and purple hair today. But there are lines of decency that wise parents must enforce.

A local school official was telling me of a junior high sports banquet he attended that was supposed to be a semi-formal affair. When he saw some sitting at the banquet wearing baseball caps backwards, he walked over to ask them to remove their caps and discovered that they were parents! He said, "It's tough to ask a person to take his hat off when it's the child's dad!"

Parents ought to see caution lights when they hear their kids claim that something will make them look "cool," or that everyone is doing it. J. Vernon McGee used to say that a majority opinion may just mean you've got a lot of fools in one place! You don't want to purposely make your child an oddball, but you do want to use the opportunities when they arise to teach him about modesty and distinctiveness.

Speech

My uncle Don came to our house one weekend to fix our tractor when I was about eight years old. As I watched him work on that tractor for hours, I also listened. He used some words I had never heard before. There was one particular curse word that he seemed to believe particularly suited the tractor—he used it frequently.

The next week when my dad and I were loading a small wagon behind the barn, we overloaded the wagon and the axle broke, causing the load to come tumbling off. I said, "Well, that—(expletive deleted)!"

When I picked myself up off the ground, I realized I had said something I shouldn't! "Dad," I whined, "I promise: I didn't know that was a bad word!"

My dad said, "You do now." I have never used that word since!

I have heard some of the foulest language spewing from the mouths of grade-school and junior-high students. Obscene gestures from young people are more and more common. What things do children pick up from you? Children should be taught at an early age that our speech is distinctive.

In today's culture, our children are bombarded from television, music, and influences at school with language, concepts, and behavior that are not fitting for a Christian. We must not only teach them what is right and wrong, but saturate them with positive examples. We must provide some positive alternatives: Christian friends, positive entertainment, Christian contemporary music.

"Let your conversation be always full of grace, seasoned with salt, so that you may know how to answer everyone" (Colossians 4:6).

Attitude

It is popular today to have a lousy attitude. It seems everyone has something to complain about, something to whine about, some grievance, some way in which they were treated unfairly or their rights were violated. "Sue him!" we shout to anyone who has been offended.

Children can get caught up in that pouting attitude if they are not corrected. They stomp to their rooms when they're thirteen and don't come out until they get their driver's licenses!

Christians should be the leaders in positive attitudes: giving people the benefit of the doubt, quick to laugh, quick to forgive, making the most of unfair situations. "And whatever you do, whether in word or deed, do it all in the name of the Lord Jesus, giving thanks to God the Father through him" (Colossians 3:17).

In Huron, Michigan, a high school football team was whipping every team they played. Two rival teams sued the winning team, alleging the Huron team had a player using extra equipment—an artificial leg. The judge found in favor of the Huron team, commending the boy for playing in spite of his handicap.

Christians should be those who inspire others with their positive attitudes. Our young people should be encouraged to have an attitude that strives for excellence. The poet wrote, "Go not where the path may lead. Go instead where there is no path, and leave a trail."

Self-Esteem

Young people will not have the strength to resist the crowd unless they have overcome their insecurities and have been taught to have a valid self-esteem. There is a lot of talk today about imparting self-esteem, but most of what is encouraged is shallow at best and often untrue.

Psychologists today tell us just to tell our children they're special and important. Teach them to look into the mirror and say, "I'm good enough and smart enough, and people like me." They have convinced many of us it is wrong to do anything that would damage someone's self-image.

That is the reason the sponsors of our local spelling bee—as I noted before—recently dropped their sponsorship of the spelling bee. They claimed it wasn't worth "destroying the self-esteem of the children who didn't win"! But life has some disappointments. Nobody wins all the time. We must begin to communicate the truth to our children regarding their self-worth, or they will never have true self-esteem.

And this is the truth: Apart from God, you are not worth very much at all. You can become the president of the company, a multimillionaire, the principal of the school, or a star athlete, but one hundred years from now very few people, if any, will know who you are. Even those who do know won't care very much.

The Bible says we are made from dust and to dust we will return (Genesis 3:19). I have preached a lot of funerals, and it always amazes me how quickly people recover. Tony Campolo says they weep over your grave, then they go back to the church and eat potato salad and laugh a lot. You are not very important to this world, and this world will get along without you pretty well when you are gone.

Solomon discovered that truth. He wrote:

Man's fate is like that of the animals; the same fate awaits them both: As one dies, so dies the other. All have the same breath; man has no advantage over the animal. Everything is meaningless (Ecclesiastes 3:19).

The only thing that gives you worth and value in this life is your relationship to God. Jesus said that apart from him we can do nothing (John 15:5). Apart from him we *are* nothing.

We recently had an auction of donated items to help raise money for a new facility. Peggy Kennedy of our church donated an old scarf. It was ugly. It had sweat stains all over it. But Peggy Kennedy knew it would be of value to someone, because it had once belonged to Elvis Presley. The sweat stains were his. It had his autograph on it. He wore it during a concert he gave in Louisville many years ago, and when he threw it out into the audience, Peggy Kennedy caught it. The scarf sold for over 700 dollars because it had once belonged to someone famous.

We have worth, not because of who we are, but because we belong to Someone of ultimate importance. We wear the bloodstains of Christ. He knows your name and the number of hairs on your head. He knows the thoughts of your heart.

> Do you not know that your body is a temple of the Holy Spirit, who is in you, whom you have received from God? You are not your own; you were bought at a price. Therefore honor God with your body (1 Corinthians 6:19, 20).

Sometimes, there is a high price to pay for being distinctive. Dietrich Bonhoffer preached against the policies of Adolph Hitler, and then was so upset by Hitler's election that he left Germany and came to America. But in the safe confines of America he felt cowardly. He said, "Someday Nazism will fall. When it does, how can I try to lead people when I fled to safety?" He returned to Germany, preached the truth, and stood almost alone. He enraged Hitler so much that he was arrested, thrown into a concentration camp, and persecuted. A few weeks before the end of the war, Bonhoffer was executed. Before he died, he wrote a classic book on being distinctive, *The Cost of Discipleship*. Dietrich Bonhoffer was distinctive.

Marcey Oglesby is distinctive, too. Marcey's eighth-grade teacher invited a counselor to come and teach the students about assertiveness in relationships. The counselor asked the students, "If your parents asked you to do the laundry and you didn't want to do it, how would you respond?"

The correct answer was supposed to be that you should assert yourself and communicate your true feelings to your parents. Marcey said, "I would obey my parents, because that's the right thing to do."

The counselor spent ten minutes of class time arguing with Marcey, trying to convince her to change her mind. The counselor asked, "What if your parents asked you to do something wrong?" It was illogical to use such a hypothetical question, and it was certainly intimidating. But Marcey did not give in.

"My parents would not ask me to do something that was wrong," Marcey claimed, and she stood her ground. Marcey may not receive a great grade in the class, but there is something more important than grades: God is pleased when we stand for the truth. Marcey's parents are pleased as well. They have taught Marcey to be distinctive.

Jesus also paid a high price for his distinctiveness. And before he died, he issued to us the challenge to be distinctive:

> If anyone would come after me, he must deny himself and take up his cross daily and follow me. For whoever wants to save his life will lose it, but whoever loses his life for me will save it. What good is it for a man to gain the whole world, and yet lose or forfeit his very self? (Luke 9:23-25).

We all know the influence parents have on children. But it is not just parents who influence children. Grandparents, uncles, aunts, neighbors, and friends all have influence. You will not know until eternity what kind of influence you have had on the next generation.

Be distinctive. Pass on the baton of faith to those young people around you.

> Set an example for the believers [especially the children] in speech, in life, in love, in faith and in purity (1 Timothy 4:12).

May all who come behind us find us faithful!

---

[1]Quoted in Charles Swindoll, *Living Above the Level of Mediocrity* (Dallas: Word, 1989).

160